BRITISH WOMEN'S COMIC FICTION, 1890–1990

To JAYNE MANGINO, *my best friend*

British Women's Comic Fiction, 1890–1990

Not Drowning, But Laughing

Margaret D. Stetz

Ashgate

Aldershot • Burlington USA • Singapore • Sydney

Published by
Ashgate Publishing Limited
Gower House
Croft Road
Aldershot
Hants GU11 3HR
England

Ashgate Publishing Company
131 Main Street
Burlington, VT 05401-5600 USA

Ashgate website: http://www.ashgate.com

British Library Cataloguing-in-Publication Data

Stetz, Margaret D.
British Women's Comic Fiction, 1890–1990: Not Drowning, But Laughing
1. Humorous stories, English – History and criticism
2. Humorous stories, English – Women authors
I. Title
823' . 00917

Library of Congress Control Number: 2001087932

ISBN 0 7546 0390 3

Printed on acid-free paper

Printed and bound by Athenaeum Press, Ltd.,
Gateshead, Tyne & Wear.

Contents

Acknowledgments

I would like to thank the *Journal of Modern Literature* for permission to reprint the part of Chapter Two which appeared in the Fall 1993 issue (XVIII, 4, 369–80), and *Studies in the Novel* for permission to reprint the part of Chapter Three which appeared in the Spring 1996 issue, v. 28 (copyright 1996 by the University of North Texas, reprinted by permission of the publisher). An earlier and shorter version of Chapter One appeared in the volume *The Victorian Comic Spirit: New Perspectives* (Ashgate, 2000), edited by Jennifer Wagner-Lawlor, to whom I am extremely grateful for introducing me to Ashgate Publishing. I thank Erika Gaffney, too, my editor at Ashgate, for all her help with this project.

For many sorts of professional and personal kindness, my thanks go to Ann Ardis, Barbara Gates, Florence Boos, Pamela Caughie, Anna Clarke, María DeGuzmán, Vanessa Dickerson, Andrea Dimino, Jessica Feldman, Leona Fisher, Steven Halliwell, Suzanne Jones, Norman Kelvin, Holly Laird, Selma Moss-Ward, Bonnie B. C. Oh, William Peterson, B. J. Robinson, Meri-Jane Rochelson, Talia Schaffer, James Slevin, Donald D. Stone, Lynn Thiesmeyer, Susan Waterman, and Linda G. Zatlin. My father, Stephen Stetz, has been unfailingly generous and supportive of me in ways that I can never repay. Steve Goodman has sustained me for years with his wonderful laughter and love. And Mark Samuels Lasner—graceful, witty, and ornamental—is my beloved collaborator in everything, forever and always.

Introduction

"Vexed," "difficult," "complicated," "problematic"—what word can sum up the history of the relationship of women to laughter, even to their own laughter? On the one hand, they have very often been the target of men's jokes. On the other, they have confronted so many cultural and political factors that have discouraged them from laughing—whether at men, at other women, or at the institutions that govern their cultures. To survey women's comic fiction in Britain alone, from the eighteenth century to the present, is to find one scene after another of female protagonists attempting, successfully or unsuccessfully, to suppress their immediate response to ridiculous circumstances or being punished in some way for not attempting to do so. Women writers of comedy it seems, have long defended their own practices in this fashion; they have created situations that will make their readers laugh, while also demonstrating, through their fictional characters' conduct, that they know it is wrong (or, at least, considered so) for women to indulge in making jokes or in showing that they find something funny. Even well into the twentieth century, women authors have had better luck in overcoming the old taboos of female chastity and modesty than the prohibitions against having women characters openly indulge a sense of humor.

This pattern in fiction established itself early, when, in 1778, Fanny Burney sent a young lady out into the world. Evelina's very first adventure turned into a misadventure, for she made the grave error not only of refusing one dancing partner at a ball in favor of another, but of laughing at the affectations of the first:

> I interrupted him—I blush for my folly,—with laughing; yet I could not help it, for, added to the man's stately foppishness, (and he actually took snuff between every three words) when I looked round at Lord Orville, I saw such extreme surprise in his face,—the cause of which appeared so absurd, that I could not for my life preserve my gravity.
>
> I had not laughed before from the time I had left Miss Mirvan, and I had much better have cried then. . . . (Burney, 33)

As Susan Staves notes, the rest of the narrative is designed to expose fops and other unwelcome social types as ridiculous, but also to teach both Evelina and the female reader not to laugh—either at these types or, it seems, at anything whatsoever. As Staves says, "All the resources of Fanny Burney's art are used to exorcise from Evelina . . . those qualities which give life to the book and to embody them in characters who are then criticized for their boldness" (Staves, 27). By the end, the comic spirit in general has vanished (and not merely the satirical in particular), both from the protagonist and from the text itself: "The more demure, more anxious regions of Fanny Burney's consciousness were appropriate to the character of a young lady heroine, but the lively, critical spirit of a satirist, which society and the marriage market found unappealing in young ladies, she disowns in the novel . . . ." (Staves, 26).

Situations in which female characters learn to be wary about when and at whom they should laugh have remained a prominent feature of women's comedies ever afterward, although similar scenes rarely have turned up in novels by and for men. Jane Austen grew up in a literate gentry culture where, according to Deborah Kaplan, not only her family, but her neighbors of both sexes engaged in witty exchanges in person and in "playful" writing and parody in their correspondence (Kaplan, 93–4). Yet Austen would feel the need to teach the protagonist of *Emma* and the audience, too, an agonizing lesson about women's responsibility to curb their wit, through the "stab of unforgettable pain when Emma . . . mocks poor harmless Miss Bates to her face" (Blythe, 27). In Elizabeth Gaskell's *Cranford* (1853), the humor-loving female narrator would hear from Miss Matty about the dreadful and irrevocable damage to the Jenkyns family caused by a prank played by her brother Peter, at whose jokes Matty formerly had been inclined to laugh. Almost a century later, Barbara Pym, whose "genius," as John Bayley has rightly remarked, "is in the art of being funny without being superior" (Bayley, 54) would nevertheless trap the heroine of *Excellent Women* (1952) in situations where she must be subjected to the hilariously inappropriate behavior of those with greater social privilege and advantages, yet feel "unable even to laugh" (Pym, 149).

Perhaps as an antidote to so much suppression of laughter, some feminist writing since the so-called Second Wave of the early 1970s has gone far in the opposite direction, championing comedy as a means toward achieving personal liberation and also as an effective political tool for the women's movement as a whole. As Nancy Walker has suggested in *A Very Serious Thing* (1988),

> The humorist is at odds with the publicly espoused values of the culture .... For women to adopt this role means that they must break out of the passive, subordinate position mandated for them by centuries of patriarchal tradition and take on the power accruing to those who reveal the shams, hypocrisies, and incongruities of the dominant culture. To be a woman and a humorist is to confront and subvert the very power that keeps women powerless .... (Walker, 9)

Gloria Kaufman has had equally laudatory things to say in favor of comedy's political potential in her two anthologies, *Pulling Our Own Strings* (1980) and *In Stitches* (1991). In the Introduction to the former, she has praised "feminist satire [which], like feminist humor, is founded on hope and predicated on a stance of nonacceptance" (Kaufman, *Pulling Our Own Strings,* 14); for her, "It is a humor based on visions of change" (13) that can be effected. In the latter volume, too, she has reaffirmed this point: "Oppressed peoples deliberately use humor to lighten the burdens of daily life so that they can survive. Feminist humor, however, is not merely (or even primarily) survival humor .... Feminist humor clarifies vision with the satiric intent of inspiring change" (Kaufman, *In Stitches,* viii). Drawing upon rhetoric that emphasizes freedom and the breaking of barriers, Frances Gray has claimed that "Women's major contribution to comic theory is, perhaps, to have stressed the importance of a laughter that does not stop, that works ceaselessly to steal the language, rebuild it and fly with it" (Gray, 185).

Meanwhile, however, Evelyn Edson has also considered comedy from a feminist perspective, yet raised doubts about its value as a political instrument. Arguing for a more skeptical view of laughter and its effects, though on very different grounds from those of Burney or Gaskell, she has speculated as to whether laughter might sometimes need to be suppressed: "At first glance, it is not so obvious that feminists should have a sense of humor. Humor can be used to defuse anger and undermine action .... Humor can help us deal with difficult situations, but may weaken the will to change them by ridiculing all effort" (Edson, 31). Comedy, as she has suggested, may sometimes serve only to reinforce the undesirable status quo.

Whether to embrace laughter affirmatively, whether to do so in a careful and limited manner, or whether to forswear it entirely—women's opinions and, indeed, feminists' opinions have seldom been in accord on an answer. And if there has been disagreement over the reception that women's comedy ought to expect, there has been just as much uncertainty when it comes to identifying that comedy in the first place and acknowledging its existence.

Much literary humor by British women of the past century has been overlooked or deliberately ignored, even by feminist readers and critics. Thus, the question of how to value this material is in some ways premature, for a large body of work still waits even to be noticed.

The present study is part of that recovery effort, focusing primarily upon comedy that has received little critical attention. Some of the choices of subject may seem eclectic or perhaps eccentric. This volume is certainly not meant to be an exhaustive (or exhausting) survey of all British women's comic fiction over the last one hundred years, but a selection of essays that illuminate cultural corners and margins and, in doing so, reflect light upon the larger landscape.

My guiding principle in assembling these chapters was to look for British women writers who were not merely producing comic texts, but who were bringing to the foreground, in their comedies, the issue of laughter as something problematic and unsettling, to be puzzled over and talked about in ethical, political, and pragmatic terms. Across the space of a century—and, in some cases, across differences of class, race, religion, ethnicity, and sexuality—these authors continue to ponder similar questions: Should women claim the right to laugh? Are there different kinds of laughter? What good does laughter do? What harm does it do? Can it do anything whatsoever?

As I looked closely at this set of British women's works, one of the hardest tasks was to decide whether what I was examining could be called "comedy" at all. Rarely, as many critics have observed, do women authors favor the medium of the joke; thus, by the standards of masculine joke-telling, their efforts may not even seem to be comic. More often, in fact, they may appear at first to be quite the reverse—if not tragic, then at least filled with painful, discomforting material. And yet, from grim situations, laughter continually emerges. In describing *Running for Their Lives* (2000), her edited collection of essays about the situations of girls around the world, Sherrie A. Inness states,

> This anthology . . . is about girls who make the best of their lives in seemingly impossible situations. It is about girls who manage to maintain their dignity, despite the indignities heaped upon them. Although these girls suffer, they also show their ability to overcome tremendous hardships. (Inness, xviii)

One could say the same about many of these comic texts by women. Despite Gloria Kaufman's reminder that "Feminist humor . . . is not merely (or even primarily) survival humor" (Kaufman, *In Stitches,* viii), survival is nonetheless an important feminist goal; there is no hope for change, unless one can first make it through the "tremendous hardships," and that is difficult enough. Creating a climate in which survival will be possible continues to be among the aims of much of the comedy written by and for women in the last one hundred years. When British women writers have weighed the power of comedy and found it wanting, it is because they have discovered its limitations in guaranteeing survival.

Nevertheless, women's laughter has broken through in unlikely places, and their works often have turned unexpectedly comic. Laura Severin, for instance, has detailed how the British woman poet, Stevie Smith, was given to bursts of "resistant antics." In her books of poetry, she would match lyrics about death and despair with line drawings very different in mood. Such was the case with her most famous poem, the 1957 "Not Waving but Drowning," which Smith accompanied with the image of "a girl . . . from the waist up, bobbing in the water. Curiously, her hair covers her face, allowing us to see only a mysterious smile" (Severin, 72–3). Severin asks why Smith would "place a picture of a seemingly satisfied girl next to a poem of a drowning man [.] The contrast could suggest that a man who ventures outside society's boundaries drowns, but a female survives and even flourishes." Therefore, Severin concludes, Smith's image of a woman smiling is a sign that "to be 'outside' brings life, not death, for women" (Severin, 73). We might go further, to say that it brings not only life, but pleasure. Many women's texts, too, might at first appear to be records of drowning, when they are actually accounts of trying to survive by staying buoyant and smiling, if not laughing.

My chronological starting point for this study is the 1890s. This was the decade when the word "feminism" first appeared in Britain and when a new self-consciousness about women's political identities entered the ongoing Victorian struggle for women's rights—a time, too, when women were ridiculed for their activism and had to decide whether or not to mock their attackers in return. The endpoint for this volume is the 1980s, when British feminism was challenged to remake itself as a newly inclusive and diverse movement, and when some of the significant debates occurred around and through the issue of comedy. In framing my study this way, I hope to make clear that I believe there have been links between moments of crisis and concern in British feminism, throughout the past century, and moments of crisis and concern over women's laughter—instances that have paired the subjects of drowning and laughing. I am not looking here at women's laughter as a "universal" or historical phenomenon, but as something integrally bound up with particular cultural events and specific political realities that have influenced authors, shaped their texts, and determined their audiences' responses.

Although this study concludes around 1990, it would be wrong to imagine that British women writers stopped laughing at that point. If anything, their comic reach has extended itself, moving increasingly into new media—out of the world of fiction and into the sphere of film, in particular. And yet, the same questions about whether laughter is or is not politically useful and ethically defensible—whether it should be celebrated or suppressed—continue to surface in women's filmed comedy. Thus, for example, *Bhaji on the Beach* (1993), written by Meera Syal and directed by Gurinder Chadha, begins with the "Saheli Asian Women's Group" going off to Blackpool to have, in the words of the community center's feminist organizer, "a female fun time." Scenes of "female fun" do occur at the seaside, involving the laughter of the group. Sometimes this laughter is directed at one of the older, more conservative members; sometimes it is an explosion of delight and surprise; sometimes it is a wry acknowledgment of shared experience, especially with British racism—but the comedy is fleeting and always threatening to dissolve into its antithesis.

In a women's bar that features white male strippers, the laughter becomes a roar and seems, at least temporarily, to connect the Asian group with the white women customers, who are also laughing. But a moment later, a stripper playfully pulls off the jacket of Ginder, one of the South Asian British women, to reveal her bruised arm, the mark of her estranged husband's battering. None of the white women present seem to see or to react to this spectacle; they go on cheering and applauding the strippers, caught up in their own sense of community and release. Only the Asian women respond to this sight or understand what it signifies, and their laughter turns to horror. Greater horror will follow at the seashore, as Ginder's husband tries to reclaim both her and their child. It will take direct and aggressive action, not laughter, on the part of the assembled women to prevent this. Their "female fun time" may allow them to enjoy a sense of shared experience, but it will not suffice to stop what threatens to turn into a violent death; ultimately, to save another's life requires other kinds of intervention and activism.

Having rescued Ginder and the child from a form of drowning, the Saheli Asian Women's Group returns from the sea, back on its bus. Laughter is restored by Rekha, a visitor from India, who unveils a souvenir made of candy—huge white breasts bearing the motto "Blackpool or Bust." But the film's final visual images are not of this laughter or of a united female circle. Instead, they show Simi, the feminist group coordinator, alone in the frame and driving the bus. Her face is in profile, outlined against the darkness of the window. She is smiling slightly, pensively, perhaps ruefully, and her smile seems to fade as the camera holds the shot. Her eyes are focused on the road ahead, as she drives into the night—not drowning, not laughing, but continuing and moving forward into the unknown future.

Clearly, the new generations of women authors who write for the good of other women will, like the members of the British feminist movement with which they often are allied, go on interrogating themselves both scrupulously and publicly about their own practices and aims. But it is just as clear that, for all their reservations, they will do what their predecessors have done for the past one hundred years and continue, at least sometimes, to laugh.

CHAPTER ONE

The Laugh of the New Woman

> You only have to look at the Medusa straight on to see her. And she's not deadly. She's beautiful and she's laughing.
>
> Hélène Cixous, "The Laugh of the Medusa" (289)

The laughing woman is the least remembered woman of the Victorian period. (Just say the words "Victorian period" and no smiling female faces will come to mind.) New Women writers are probably the least remembered authors of the Victorian period. And so—to follow out this formula—those New Women writers who employed the comic mode are the most forgotten among the forgotten, their jests at the expense of patriarchal ideologies and institutions lost to readers today, and even to most feminist scholars. You will not find their comedy discussed in studies of New Women's fiction, such as Ann Ardis's *New Women, New Novels* (1990), Rita Kranidis's *Subversive Discourse* (1995), Sally Ledger's *The New Woman* (1997), Ann Heilmann's *New Woman Fiction* (2000), or Angelique Richardson and Chris Willis's edited volume, *The New Woman in Fiction and Fact* (2001). Neither do they receive a mention in recent works on feminist comedy, such as Frances Gray's *Women and Laughter* (1994) or the two volumes of essays edited by Regina Barreca, *Last Laughs* (1988) and *New Perspectives on Women and Comedy* (1992). Even Ada Leverson, a New Woman who was perhaps the best known female satirist of the 1890s, has been shut out entirely from *The Penguin Book of Women's Humor* (1996), a volume billed on its back cover as "a landmark anthology . . . [with] extravagantly wide-ranging selections . . . [that] span three centuries." (Fortunately, her 1890s parodies and comic pieces have been rescued lately from total neglect by Margaret Debelius, in an essay titled "Countering a Counterpoetics: Ada Leverson and Oscar Wilde.")

Yet, though the peculiar character of the New Woman's laughter remains unexplored, there is much to be learned from it. It teaches us both about the strategies that women have used in times of assault upon themselves and upon their work and about their hesitations and reservations when taking up forms identified with the exercise of masculine prerogative. The example of New Woman comic writers can certainly show us comedy's function as a survival tactic, but also the limits of its effectiveness in forwarding change—an effectiveness that our feminist predecessors were right to doubt and question.

Conservative male contemporaries may have feared the rebellious will of the New Woman and regarded her personally as so sinister and destructive a figure that she would have to be ridiculed into submission, if not physically clubbed. The evidence suggests, nevertheless, that when New Women writers actually took up a cultural weapon such as the cudgel of laughter, they wielded it with some ambivalence, conscious of its problematic and double-edged nature. In studying Leverson's parodies, Margaret Debelius has concluded that such comedy of the 1890s "sheds light on fin-de-siècle women writers' ambivalent and often contradictory attitude toward literary cultural decadence" (Debelius, 193). But I would like to go further, to suggest that it also sheds light on their "contradictory attitude" toward laughter itself.

Although they were often portrayed by their detractors as man-slaying monsters, the New Women of the 1890s—like the transformed icons of Hélène Cixous's 1975 essay, "Le Rire de la Méduse,"—appear, when looked at "straight on," not to have been so "deadly" at all in their intentions (Cixous, 289). In fact, the comedy authored by New Women and their supporters was, in general, far less vituperative and fierce than the comedy directed at them. Is this discrepancy a sign that the New Women writers—many of whom were members of the middle classes and thus burdened with the training appropriate to "ladies"—were too timid, too repressed, or just too nice to fight fire with fire? Perhaps. My own research, however, suggests that their avoidance of no-holds-barred satire did not merely represent unconscious feminine discomfort with aggression, but also a conscious rejection of such masculine posturing, both on moral and on practical grounds. Though their antagonists may have believed that driving these newly self-assertive and noisy women back into submission and silence through intimidation by ridicule would put the world right again, New Women of the Nineties were too clearsighted to imagine that merely laughing at men or at male-generated institutions would solve their difficulties.

In the long run, the New Women proved to be correct in their assessment of comedy's limitations. After all, the lampoons of turn-of-the-century feminism that circulated regularly, both in the popular press and in the intellectual sphere of High Art, were insufficient to destroy the women's movement or to squelch its growing demands. Ridicule may have been an effective weapon for inflicting injury, but it could not deliver a fatal blow. New Women writers did laugh and did attempt to make their readers laugh, but their attitude toward laughter, unlike that of their adversaries, was complex and rooted in skepticism. Laughter was, for them, only one element of social and psychological liberation or of political action, and a somewhat unreliable one at that. It might help some women to survive, but it could not be counted upon to do the same for all women or to change the larger framework of gender politics.

I

As Sandra Gilbert and Susan Gubar have rightly described them in *War of the Words,* the first volume of their *No Man's Land,* the closing decades of the nineteenth century were a time of "women's invasion of the public sphere," when female movement out of the realm of domesticity and silence was perceived by many male observers as "an act of aggression that inaugurated a battle of the sexes" (Gilbert and Gubar, 65). By the 1890s in England, a change too great to be ignored was occurring: "[N]ever before had women been so visible in British society and culture—and hardly since, either, until the 1970s and the new women's movement" (Bjørhovde, 4). Accompanying this growing prominence of women—though particularly of middle-class women—was a masculine backlash that struck out first at the most obvious instigator of this change, the so-called "New Woman," she who was most conscious of and vocal about the injustice of present-day social and sexual hierarchies. Not merely in England, but throughout the Continent and in the United States, as well, as Elaine Showalter reminds readers in *Sexual Anarchy: Gender and Culture at the Fin de Siècle,* "the New Woman, university-educated and sexually independent, engendered intense hostility and fear as she seemed to challenge male supremacy in art, the professions, and the home" (Showalter, 38).

In the period between 1880 and 1900, the bolts drawn down by this cultural lightning-rod often took the form of derisive laughter, satire, and caricature. As Patricia Marks has documented in her study, *Bicycles, Bangs, and Bloomers,* the popular press on both sides of the Atlantic was especially virulent in its comic attacks, hoping to shame and to "tame the rambunctious feminist spirit and return it to its domestic sphere" (Marks, 2). "Images of unsightly harridans," according to Ann Heilmann, were designed to "destabilize more positive textual explorations of the New Woman" in female-authored fiction (Heilmann, 16). Male cartoonists, in particular (and most professional cartoonists and caricaturists of the nineteenth century were male) often used the charge of female humorlessness as a weapon to make the New Woman unappealing in the public's eye, as they depicted hatchet-faced, scowling sourpusses going about the business of winning equal rights. But even such a better-informed and sporadically sympathetic figure as the English novelist, George Gissing, would assert in his 1898 study of Charles Dickens that women—the New and the more familiar ones alike—were deficient in the all-important comic spirit, and that a "humourist never strongly appeals to that audience" (Gissing, 131–2).

Looking back, just a few years later, upon the heyday of the New Women of the 1890s, C. E. Lawrence would entitle an essay "Wanted—Humourists" and carry the same charge into a new century. Begging for an antidote to the recent female "nastiness," when "those mouthing animals misbehaved, and were proud of it," Lawrence would opine that "It was all as depressing as cold tea after a funeral. An ill-year for literature and fun! The Woman Who Did frowned, and humour fled. That achievement was the one triumph of Mrs. Morbidly-Neurotic" (Lawrence, 551). Women in general and feminists in particular, at the close of the nineteenth century, were allegedly too psychologically unbalanced to appreciate the sanity and healthfulness of jokes. This "requirement that they achieve 'humor'"—as well as appreciate it at their own expense, no matter how malicious or malevolent the joke—was, as Talia Schaffer has pointed out, a matter directly related to gender and to the desire for women's writings to confine themselves to a place of inferiority. "Humor was apparently a peculiarly female requirement: nobody accused Hardy of lacking it. Humor signaled the writer's light, charming point of view, which guaranteed that the work would not have serious political ideas or literary pretensions. The humor requirement was a way of demanding that women's literature be second-rate . . . ." (Schaffer, 8).

The British New Woman writer of the end of the century was forced into self-consciousness, therefore, about how she positioned herself on the issue of laughter. She faced, on the one hand, a variety of misogynistic comic attacks upon her goals and programs, whether those involved reform of the marriage laws, access to higher education and entry into the professions for women, the end of the class system, or the abolition of the double standard in sexual morality. In addition, she met with satirical portraits of herself designed to make her seem personally ridiculous—loathesome of face and deformed in body. And then, moreover, she found herself decried as incapable by nature of laughter of her own—humorless, without wit, unable to address a reader except through harangues or angry sputters. Thus when Arthur Rickett, the English literary satirist, published in 1895 "Miss Maud's Three Notes," his parody of a New Woman-ish volume of short stories titled *Keynotes* by "George Egerton" (Mary Chavelita Dunne), he depicted the feminist heroine as a grim and violent creature, hurling a flower-pot at a random man and ranting incoherently, "'I feel,' said Maud, 'I don't know—I can't express—I hate men; I loathe men. I don't know why, but I do'" (Rickett, 14–15).

According to the opposition, the greatest error of such a New Woman was her refusal to keep these sentiments to herself and her insistence instead upon making them public, even turning them to literary purposes. Her pretensions to authorship, however, were inevitably a mere nuisance or joke, as Rickett made clear in a further squib from 1895, "The New Cinderella. An Up-to-Date Fairy Tale." There is scarcely a more foolish character in the literature of the 1890s than Rickett's female protagonist, who decides, on the advice of her fairy godmother, to write novels—"turgid prose full of asterisks and hysterics"—just as all the other New Women do, and who then produces "a sickly exotic of first-class morbidness" (Rickett, 66).

But a woman did not have to consider or publicly label herself "New" in order to experience the scourge of masculine wit; indeed, "George Egerton" (Mary Chavelita Dunne), the target of Rickett's laughter, as well as of a two-part anonymous parody in *Punch* (10 March and 17 March 1894) and a separate visual caricature (*Punch,* 28 April 1894), denied repeatedly in published interviews that her work concealed any socio-political agenda or that she herself was associated in any way with those she called the "advanced" and the "unsexed." To merit lampoons or worse, nonetheless, it was enough for a female author merely to seem wilful and uncompliant to the male observer, and thus to be a fellow-traveller. So keen, in fact, was this comic scrutiny of female temperament and actions throughout the 1890s that it went beyond consideration of actual women. Even fictional characters from earlier Victorian literature were subject to retrospective judgment and punishment, as a warning to all contemporary transgressors of the ongoing rule of female subordination.

Perhaps the most extraordinary example of how this climate of ridicule extended itself in diffuse and unexpected directions, for the purpose of intimidating both the New Woman and her less political sisters who might have been tempted to air their own grievances, can be found in George Gissing's

Charles Dickens. This 1898 volume on the works of Dickens, issued in Blackie & Son's "Victorian Era Series," was at once an encomium of past satires of women and an exercise in 1890's-style misogyny. For Gissing, whose ambivalence ran so deep that it produced both tremendously sympathetic portrayals of feminists in *The Odd Women* (1893) and vicious displays of contempt for assertive, ambitious women in *The Whirlpool* (1897), this study became the occasion for justifying his fiercest prejudices by linking them with the attitudes of his esteemed literary predecessor.

Gissing noted with pleasure the mockery of a "gallery of foolish, ridiculous, or offensive women" (133) in Dickens's novels:

> For . . . it is obvious that Dickens wrote of women in his liveliest spirit of satire. Wonderful as fact, and admirable as art, are the numberless pictures of more or less detestable widows, wives, and spinsters which appear throughout his books. Beyond dispute, they must be held among his finest work; this portraiture alone would establish his claim to greatness. (133)

It was Gissing's argument, in *Charles Dickens,* that what had always been viewed as a deliberate comic distortion in the satirical portraits of women—a heightening of the characters' ridiculous traits for the sake of laughter—was nothing of the sort. On the contrary, Dickens was practicing the strictest truth-to-life, as rigorous as that of any latter-day French Naturalist:

> Here—I cannot remind the reader too often of this fact in regard to Dickens's women—one discerns absolutely nothing of "exaggeration"; not a word, not a gesture, goes beyond the very truth. Here the master would have nothing to learn from later art; he is the realist's exemplar. (155)

Dickens was, for Gissing, "the social historian of his day" (154), who recorded from experience, rather than created or enhanced, the defects present in his female characters: "Dickens must have been in constant observation of these social pests . . . . His women use utterance such as no male genius could have invented . . ." (135). And the test of Dickens's artistry was the likeness between such portraits and what, according to Gissing, a dispassionate scientific "inquirer" of the present, a figure such as the author himself, would perceive about actual women around him: "There needs no historical investigation to ascertain the truthfulness of these presentments . . . . [for] such women may be observed to-day by an inquirer sufficiently courageous; they are a multitude that no man can number . . ." (134).

Having established, then, to his own satisfaction that there was no distinction between misogynist satire and sober truth, Gissing felt free in *Charles Dickens* to indulge his comic inclinations at the expense of noisy, demanding women, conflating his descriptions of Dickens's female characters with his own malicious flights of fancy:

> In the highways and by-ways of life, by the fireside, and in the bed-chamber, their voices shrill upon the terrified ear. It is difficult to believe that death can stifle them; one imagines them upon the threshold of some other world, sounding confusion among unhappy spirits who hoped to have found peace. (133–4)

In none of these satirical passages did Gissing ever fix upon the New Women of his own time by name, as representing the latter-day equivalents of Dickens's obstreperous shrews. Nevertheless, by singling out for opprobrium those very characteristics in a woman—restlessness, loudness, immodesty, neglect of housekeeping, defiance, and discontent—for which his rebellious female contemporaries were being publicly vilified in the press, he encouraged the reader to make that identification for him. As he said of Dickens's women, employing criticisms unmistakably similar to those used against New Women of the middle-classes,

> In general their circumstances are comfortable; they suffer no hardship . . . nothing is asked of them but a quiet and amiable discharge of household duties; they are treated by their male kindred with great, often with extraordinary, consideration.
>
> Yet their characteristic is acidity of temper and boundless license of querulous or insulting talk. (133)

The connection between the comic literature of the past and the sexual politics of the present deepened, moreover, as Gissing moved the chapter called "Women and Children" toward a serious discussion of both Dickens's and his own "ideal" woman—a figure who contrasted in every way with the so-called emancipated female of the Nineties:

> I have left her [Ruth Pinch] to the last, because she will serve us as the type of all that Dickens really admired in woman. Truth to tell, it was no bad ideal. Granted that the world must go on very much in the old way, that children must be born and looked after, that dinners must be cooked, that houses must be kept sweet, it is hard to see how Ruth Pinch can ever be supplanted . . . . [To have a] little house, a little garden, the cooking her own

> peculiar care, a little maid for the little babies—this is her dream. But never, within those walls, a sound of complaining or of strife, never a wry face, acidly discontented with the husband's doings or sayings. Upon my word—is it a bad ideal? (161–2)

In contrast to the sugary tone of this brief tribute to the traditional housewife—the "thoroughly kind-hearted and home-loving woman" (161)—was the vitriol of Gissing's extended satirical attack, which filled the rest of the "Women and Children" chapter, upon those Dickensian females guilty of kicking against their domestic circumstances. Over the head of Mrs. Varden from *Barnaby Rudge*, for instance, he poured a torrent of sarcasm for the crime of poisoning her household with "persistent sourness and sulkiness" (137):

> She has in perfection all the illogicality of thought, all the maddening tricks of senseless language, which, doubtless for many thousand of years, have served her like for weapons. It is an odd thing that evolution has allowed the persistence of this art, for we may be quite sure that many a primitive woman paid for it with a broken skull. Here it is, however, flourishing and like to flourish. (137)

In commentary such as this, George Gissing and those of his masculine contemporaries who shared his dislike and distrust of unsubmissive women seemed to be establishing a new precedent for turn-of-the-century comedy. Earlier Victorian theorists had defended satirical portraiture as a mode of inciting the "correction" of its victims' manners, the kind of correction that one sees, for instance, in the male protagonist of George Meredith's "The Case of General Ople and Lady Camper" (1877), who is stung to self-improvement by the scathing caricatures of him produced by the story's artistic heroine. It was for this reason that Meredith had spoken of satire, in his 1877 essay called "On the Idea of Comedy and of the Uses of the Comic Spirit," as a form of "hard-hitting, with a moral purpose to sanction it" (Meredith, 42). Much of the misogynistic comedy of the 1890s, however, was notable for its attacks not upon manners but upon what it labelled "woman's nature," which it blamed for such eruptions as the New Woman's insurgent spirit. Deeming this condition quite incorrigible, end-of-the-century theorists advocated a kind of comedy that practiced pure assault-for-assault's sake, meant to dispose of, rather than to educate and amend, the nuisance at hand.

Thus in his study of Charles Dickens, Gissing praised the depiction of Mrs. Gargery from *Great Expectations* as capturing precisely the "shrew of the most highly developed order," whose obnoxious complaining is entirely unprovoked, groundless, and unchangeable: "Cause there is none . . . . It is the peculiarity of these women that no one can conjecture why they behave so ill. The nature of the animals—nothing more can be said" (143). But while revelling in the laughter aimed at her type, George Gissing could not be content with ridicule alone to do what Meredith had referred to as "hard-hitting," and a more blatant call to arms accompanied his jibes. In his remarks upon the female character's fate, Gissing made plain the violence and malignity that underlay many of the comic attacks upon women in the Nineties, as well as the readiness of some male authors to move beyond the text into action:

> Mrs. Gargery shall be brought to quietness; but how? By a half-murderous blow on the back of her head, from which she will never recover. Dickens understood by this time that there is no other efficacious way with these ornaments of their sex. A felling and stunning and all but killing blow, followed by paralysis and slow death. A sharp remedy, but no whit sharper than the evil it cures. (143)

Obviously, the animosity and antagonism that fuelled misogynist satire in the 1890s did not go unremarked by its victims. But the comedy produced in turn by New Women of the period seldom went for the kill. More often, it kept intact the Meredithian tradition of using laughter merely to inspire change and improvement. The satire that it favored was usually limited and localized in its targets—not "the nature of the animal" for "many thousands of years," but the particular conduct of present-day men and male-dominated institutions. Its tone, moreover, was often temperate—a version of ridicule moderate enough to allow for continued relations between the jokester and the object of mockery. And indeed, in a world where men would continue to wield greater economic and cultural power long after the laughter had died away, no New Woman with an ounce of pragmatism could afford to alienate her masculine targets completely.

A good example of the tempered and more carefully focused comedy of the New Woman was "The Last Ditch," from E. [Edith] Nesbit's *A Pomander of Verse*. E. Nesbit's volume of poetry was issued in 1895 by the Bodley Head, a firm strongly associated with New Women's texts in general, especially by authors such as "Victoria Crosse," Netta Syrett, and Evelyn Sharp. As a founding member in the 1880s of the Fabian Society, Nesbit had long been acquainted, thanks to the climate of debate around the socialist movement, with the rhetoric of anger and abuse; certainly, she could have drawn such weaponry from the arsenal of memory in order to write satire, had she so wished. What she published instead was a wry comedy with a feminist slant—an address to a coercive male lover who is an aesthete and who has fixed notions of how women ought to conform to the visions of men, especially those of popular painters and illustrators:

Love, through your varied views on Art
  Untiring have I followed you,
Content to know I had your heart
  And was your Art-ideal, too.

As, dear, I was when first we met.
  ('Twas at the time you worshipped Leighton,
And were attempting to forget
  Your Foster and your Noel Paton.)

"Love rhymes with Art," said your dear voice,
  And, at my crude, uncultured age,
I could but blushingly rejoice
  That you had passed the Rubens stage.

When Madox Brown and Morris swayed
  Your taste, did I not dress and look
Like any Middle Ages maid
  In an illuminated book?

I wore strange garments, without shame,
  Of formless form and toneless tones,
I might have stepped out of the frame
  Of a Rossetti or Burne-Jones.

I stole soft frills from Marcus Stone,
  My waist wore Herkomer's disguise,
My slender purse was strained, I own,
  But—my silk lay as Sargent's lies.

And when you were abroad—in Prague—
  'Mid Cherets I had shone, a star;
Then for your sake I grew as vague
  As Mr[.] Whistler's ladies are.

But now at last you sue in vain,
  For here a life's submission ends:

Not even for you will I grow plain
As Aubrey Beardsley's "lady friends."

Here I renounce your hand—unless
You find your Art-ideal elsewhere;
I will not wear the kind of dress
That Laurence Housman's people wear!

(Nesbit, *Pomander,* 83–4)

The speaker of "The Last Ditch" does not rail against patriarchy or against heterosexual power hierarchies in general. Neither does she complain about the burden—not even about the economic burden upon her "slender purse"—of having to fashion and refashion her appearance, while obliterating her individuality, to suit the masculine lover's shifting artistic whims. Instead, her only objection is to his latest enthusiasm: a taste for a new mode that offends her own aesthetic sense and feminine pride by making women homely. Thus, the immediate comic target of the poem is the lover's one particular excess—a specific and corrigible fault; its long-range target, rather than being any general deficiency in the attitude of men, is the grotesque stylization practiced by British illustrators of the Nineties. And even this seeming poke at contemporary masculinist British art turns out to be more of a sly, in-house dig among colleagues, delivered by someone who expects to maintain connections with the butts of her joke. In 1895, the year when "The Last Ditch" appeared, E. Nesbit, Laurence Housman, and Aubrey Beardsley were, in fact, all under contract at the Bodley Head (though Beardsley, unbeknownst to Nesbit at this point, would very soon be dropped by the firm in the wake of the Oscar Wilde scandal). Indeed, *A Pomander of Verse,* the volume containing this apparently anti-Decadent-art poem, was designed by Housman himself, complete with a title-page illustration of an attenuated female figure; moreover, when the poem was published, Nesbit had every reason to believe that her forthcoming collection of stories, *In Homespun,* for the Bodley Head's "Keynotes Series," would feature covers, spine, and title-page by Beardsley, who was in charge of the series's format.

As a group, New Women writers tended not to expend their energies on abusive and alienating forms of satire, favoring instead a version of humor that recognized the inevitability of an ongoing relationship with the masculine objects of their laughter, as well as the need to reform and improve the character of that relationship. This was not merely a reflection of some inherent female preference, of the kind that the sociolinguists such as Deborah

Tannen have identified, for joketelling that increases a jokester's "affiliation" and "intimacy" with others. It was, rather, an acknowledgment of the fact that women's comedy in the 1890s had to remain palatable to a male audience in order to achieve publication at all. (In the case of Nesbit's poem, this meant gaining the approval first of a male publisher's reader, the writer Richard Le Gallienne, who was himself a social acquaintance of both Beardsley and Housman, and then of a male publisher, John Lane, at the Bodley Head.) It was, further, grounded in the recognition that social change on either a narrow or a broad scale still depended upon the cooperation of men, who held the reins of power.

At the same time, however, that New Women were creating their own versions of comedies in the Nineties, they were consciously exploring, both in criticism and in fiction, the issue of laughter in general, sometimes approaching it from a theoretical standpoint and sometimes in terms of consequences for the individual woman who laughs. Their concerns were ethical and also practical, arising out of questions not only as to whether ridicule of men and of a masculinist culture might be just, but whether it did a woman any good or perhaps even exposed her to greater misery. The jeers and sneers directed at the New Women themselves had done nothing to reconcile them to the point of view of their attackers, so there was little reason for them to believe unconditionally in such weapons as effective political strategies for bringing about institutional change. Instead, since comedy had first presented itself in a problematic form to them, used in targeting and humiliating women, they continued to see laughter in all its guises, from scathing mockery to mere wry smiles, as a problem requiring careful scrutiny.

We can begin to get a sense of the range of turn-of-the-century women's philosophical positions on the issues surrounding laughter by contrasting the responses of two prominent female commentators, Alice Meynell and Laura Marholm (Hansson), each of whom moved into and out of the flexible and somewhat unstable category of "New Womanhood" at various points. The purpose of their arguments differed: in Meynell's case, to object to the injustice of what had passed as masculine wit and humor and to reclaim comedy as women's province, too; in Marholm's, to uncover the well-hidden tradition of women's laughter at men that did not express itself chiefly in literary texts, but also to raise troubling questions about how much this female laughter could accomplish in any case. What these critics shared was an acute sensitivity to the role of masculine comedy in supporting and maintaining unequal power relations between men and women and a moral revulsion against the infliction of pain through laughter, as well as a deep skepticism about the possibility of changing the power balance merely by reversing the gender of the joke's practitioner and the joke's victim.

Alice Meynell, the British Roman Catholic poet, may be better known now for her lyrical verse, but she was also a literary and social critic who used the platform of her essays to "be sarcastic on the subject of those men who were themselves sarcastic on the subject of women" (Sackville-West, 22). In both her private and public life, she voluntarily played out traditional feminine roles. She was, as Vita Sackville-West described her in a 1947 essay, "womanly . . . [in] her clothes, her manner, her quiet assumption of her right as a woman towards whom homage was due . . . ." (Sackville-West, 21), as well as in the way that she took on the identities of "mother" and "hostess" (Sackville-West, 21). Nevertheless, her own New Woman-ish sympathies came through in an essay such as "A Woman in Grey" from *The Colour of Life* (1896), her paean to the female bicyclist as the embodiment of "watchful confidence," female "courage," readiness to assume "equal risk," and ability to overcome having been as a "woman . . . long educated to sit still" (Meynell, *Colour,* 68–71). But most of all, her feminist spirit of dissatisfaction with the social order of the day exercised itself in protests against the disrepectful treatment of women by male writers.

In an essay titled "Laughter" that was collected in her 1909 volume, *Ceres' Runaway and Other Essays,* Alice Meynell would note with displeasure the efforts of her turn-of-the-century male contemporaries to arrogate to themselves the right to decide what was funny:

> There is, in a word, a determination, an increasing tendency . . . [for] laughter [to be] everywhere and at every moment proclaimed to be the honourable occupation of men, and in some degree distinctive of men, and no mean part of their prerogative and privilege. The sense of humour is chiefly theirs, and those who are not men are to be admitted to the jest upon their explanation. (Meynell, "Laughter," 30)

Such a situation, as Meynell had stated in an earlier meditation on the subject of laughter titled "Penultimate Caricature," left the female spectator in a difficult position—not only excluded from the process of defining the comic, but, in some cases, subject to scorn for even daring to point out the implications of a so-called "jest." As she wrote in that essay in 1893, "Obviously to make a serious comment on anything which others consider or have considered humorous is to put one's-self at a disadvantage. He who sees the joke holds himself somewhat the superior . . . " (Meynell, *Rhythm,* 101).

Meynell risked placing herself at a disadvantage, nonetheless, in order to protest against what she identified as a continuing trend of "derision of the woman" in nineteenth-century culture (*Rhythm,* 105). She began "Penultimate Caricature," the essay to which she gave the honor of closing her 1893 volume called *The Rhythm of Life,* with an acknowledgment that hers was a minority position, for she was taking exception to a characteristic of earlier Victorian art by which few evidently had been troubled: "There has been no denunciation, and perhaps even no recognition, of a certain social immorality in the caricature of the mid-century and earlier. Literary and pictorial alike, it had for its notice the vulgarising of the married woman" (101). Preceding Gissing's book on Dickens by just five years, Meynell's essay singled out Dickens and some of his contemporaries (including Jerrold, Leech, and Keene)—not, this time, for praise, but rather for tough critical scrutiny. In Gissing's eyes, Dickens could do no wrong as a satirist. But were these mid-Victorians, Meynell asked, really models worthy of emulation by artists of the Nineties? In their works, she found what seemed to her both unfair and unwarranted expressions of disgust at women's conduct and at their physical bodies, especially in their role as wives:

> There is in some old Punch volume a drawing by Leech . . . where the work of the artist has vied with the spirit of the letter-press. Douglas Jerrold treats of the woman's jealousy, Leech of her stays. They lie on a chair by the bed, beyond description gross. And page by page the woman is derided, with an unfailing enjoyment of her foolish ugliness of person, of manners, and of language. (102)

The word that she chose to describe such proceedings was an interesting one. In 1893, at a time when male critics reserved the use of "immorality" almost exclusively for their descriptions of contemporary European and British Naturalism and for novels by New Women writers, Meynell applied it not to literary offenses against the prevailing code of sexual propriety but, more daringly, to offenses against the good name of Woman.

As might be expected, Meynell's portrait of Charles Dickens in the essay "Penultimate Caricature" differed radically from the one Gissing would draw soon afterward in his own critical sketch. For Meynell, Dickens was not at all the "social historian," whose satires of women approached in technique the scientific accuracy of the later French realism and whose example, therefore, could be used to validate all subsequent attacks upon women's existence; he was instead an artist with a dreadful blind spot that made him treat his female subjects unjustly:

> In that time there was, moreover, one great humourist; he bore his part willingly in vulgarising the woman; and the part that fell to him was the vulgarising of the act of maternity. Woman spiteful . . . woman incoherent, woman abandoned without restraint to violence and temper . . . in none of these ignominies is woman so common, foul, and foolish for Dickens as she is in child-bearing. (102–3)

It would have been clear to Meynell's audience that her intention in this essay was not to malign Dickens's reputation or to suggest that his novels made unsuitable reading, even for women. Indeed, there is no sign either here or in her later essay titled "Dickens," from the 1917 collection *Hearts of Controversy,* of the antipathy toward his work that George Gissing would attribute to female readers in general, because of their alleged lack of a sense of humor (Gissing, 131–2). On the contrary, Dickens was, for Meynell, a writer whose inspiration often seemed to have been "celestial" and whose creations were sometimes "ultimately to be traced, through Dickens, to God" (Meynell, "Dickens," 110). And while announcing her admiration for his skill at "dramatic tragedy" ("Dickens," 110), she insisted even more strongly that "it be granted that Dickens the humourist is foremost and most precious" ("Dickens," 117). Her unhappiness was solely with his choice of targets, and her criticism of Dickens's comedy remained a precise and local one, focused only upon his denial of fair treatment to women.

But the aim of Alice Meynell's criticism in "Penultimate Caricature" was not merely to blast the tastes in satire of Englishmen fifty years earlier; rather, as was evident from the conclusion toward which this essay built, its purpose lay in addressing the present day and in shaping future literary and social practices. Referring boldly again to misogyny as an ethical crime, Meynell finished by noting that "This great immorality, centring in the irreproachable days of the Exhibition of 1851, or thereabouts—the pleasure in this particular form of human disgrace" was still clearly traceable in her contemporaries, especially in the "habit by which some men reproach a silly woman through her sex, whereas a silly man is not reproached through his sex" (*Rhythm,* 106). Meynell's method of dealing with this current injustice was a subtle one: to create in her readers a revulsion against the misogynistic excesses of the past that could make them wish to change their own behavior. And by allowing the audience first to recognize the evils of sexism in comic art from which it felt some detachment or distance—such as that produced by the passage of forty or fifty years—she could lessen the sense of personal threat that a male reader, in particular, might experience in the face of an example closer to home.

Meynell's tactics were those of a moderate, but that does not mean that they were determined purely by considerations of what might reach or might placate a male audience. Her arguments also made their appeal to those women readers of the Nineties who, frightened off by the hostile caricatures in *Punch* and other journals of middle-class opinion, had become reluctant to identify themselves with the more direct protests of the New Women against contemporary manifestations of woman-hating, but who could safely second a criticism of mid-Victorian forebearers. Such women—though not so bold as those who identified themselves with the movements for the radical overhaul of the gender system—also suffered from a feeling of physical and spiritual humiliation, which they had no outlet for expressing, whenever they encountered representations of female "grossness." For these middle-class female readers of the *Pall Mall Gazette,* the *Scots Observer,* and other periodicals in which her essays first appeared, Meynell served as a welcome and unthreatening defender of women's rights.

Female critics of the 1890s produced a wide spectrum of response, both to the pressing issue of male ridicule of women and to the problems attaching themselves to the concept of laughter as a whole. Clearly, Meynell's reactions came down on the side of optimism and potential for reform; her complaints about masculine satires of women were meant to inaugurate a process of change, first in artistic representations and then in life. But not all feminist theorists seemed to believe in such a hopeful outcome. Very different in tone and in underlying assumptions were the writings, for instance, of Laura Marholm (Hansson). Her book-length study called *Modern Women*—issued in 1896 by John Lane, the Bodley Head, publisher of much New Woman literature, in a translation from German by Hermione Ramsden—appeared in England at a moment when public events had revealed the vicious and sadistic undercurrent running through laughter in general at the end of the century. Only months before, on the afternoon of 21 November 1895, Oscar Wilde had stood on a railway platform at Clapham Junction, waiting to be transferred by his jailers to Reading prison. "Handcuffed and in prison clothing," the most celebrated comic playwright of the decade, having been convicted on charges of "gross indecency" for homosexual activity, met his audience:

"A crowd formed, first laughing and then jeering at him. One man recognized that this was Oscar Wilde, and spat at him" (Ellmann, 465).

The outbursts of extreme malevolence that seemed to arise especially around the issues of gender roles and sexuality and that expressed itself through ridicule were hardly confined to England in this period. In a second volume of literary criticism published by the Bodley Head in 1899, *We Women and Our Authors,* Laura Marholm would title one of her chapters "The Women-Haters, Tolstoy and Strindberg" and would devote much of her discussion of the latter figure to recording how, in his representations of women, he could "never depict them ludicrously and repulsively enough" to satisfy himself (Marholm, *We Women,* 160). Marholm, an author who was "a German-speaking Dano-Russian from Latvia with Norwegian relatives" (Brantly, 5), spent much time in Denmark and in Sweden with her husband, the Swedish writer Ola Hansson. Thus, she became well aware of the relationship, at least in Northern European and Scandinavian culture at the turn of the century, between masculine anger and ridicule directed against women and the upsurge of feminist political agitation. As she noted in placing Strindberg's plays of the 1880s and 1890s in their political context:

> In the course of a few years there appeared a collection of dramas evincing a hatred of woman quite unparalleled in the literature of the world. It was just at the time when the Scandinavian movement for the emancipation of women was in full swing, with its natural accompaniment of women authors . . . . (Hansson, *We Women,* 169–70)

Yet, even though Laura Marholm fervently condemned misogyny, whether masked as comedy or not, her own support of the "movement for the emancipation of women" proved ambivalent and wavering. Her intellectual stance throughout the Nineties was a deliberately provocative one, yoking together elements of the New Woman and the so-called "Womanly Woman" arguments in an irresolvable tension. A believer in essentialism and in biology as destiny, she claimed that "Owing to her physiological structure woman is a creature of instinct," born with an "unfathomable . . . incomprehensible nature" that produces an "utter disregard for law and justice and all the rest of the intricate building of commonsense upon which human society is founded" (*We Women,* 56); thus, any demand that women be given a university education, the vote, or training for intellectual careers was, to her, fundamentally misguided. But while extolling the glories of female "instinct" and condemning those who would educate women for the professions, Marholm displayed more than her share of "commonsense," as well as a learned acquaintance with contemporary literature and philosophy from across Europe and an unquenchable ambition to see her own writings published and taken seriously. This divided temperament made her a fitting mediator, however, between more conservative women readers and the New Women writers—the role that she created for herself in the 1896 volume called *Modern Women*. It was, indeed, in the capacity of a kind of feminist go-between that she appeared in the chapter from *Modern Women* titled "Neurotic Keynotes," offering reflections inspired by her reading of two volumes of short stories (*Keynotes* from 1893 and *Discords* from 1894, both published by the Bodley Head) by the Irish writer, "George Egerton" (Mary Chavelita Dunne).

Throughout that chapter, Marholm's discussion of the comedy of heterosexual relations became an occasion for expressing her ambivalent view of women's position under patriarchy. She was, on the one hand, strongly attracted to the concept of femininity as a form of power to be exercised and enjoyed—something that gave women the ability to tease, manipulate, control, and, especially, to mock men. But she was also aware of the restrictions on that power imposed by the economic and political disparities of gender. And, most of all, she felt enormous sympathy for those women who began by using the advantage of feminine laughter in their dealings with men, only to find themselves yoked eventually in marriage to men whom they could not respect and who would not respect them, locked forever in a socially sanctioned arrangement where their so-called "feminine advantages" could do them no good.

The conflicts between these notions of female power and powerlessness begin to emerge as Marholm describes the secret comic perspective of women, which rarely finds representation in literary form:

> It is almost universal amongst women, especially Germans, that they do not take men as seriously as he likes to imagine. They think him comical . . . . Men have no idea what a comical appearance they present, not only as individuals, but as a race. The comic part about a man is that he is so different from women, and that is just what he is proudest of. The more refined and fragile a woman is, the more ridiculous she is likely to find the clumsy, great creature, who takes such a roundabout way to gain his comical ends. To young girls especially, man offers a perpetual excuse for a laugh, and a secret shudder. When men find a group of women laughing among themselves, they never suspect that it is they who are the cause of it. And that again is so comic. The better a man is, the more he is in earnest when he makes his pathetic appeal for a great love, and woman, who takes

> a special delight in playing a little false, even when there is no necessity, becomes as earnest and solemn as he, when all the time she is only making fun of him. (*Modern Women,* 64–5)

Marholm outlines a scenario in which women can counter masculine supremacy and dominate men through their laughter—a triumph all the greater, because it occurs without the victim's knowledge. Only recently, she asserts, has the literary evidence of this mocking attitude toward men finally appeared, in the short stories published as *Keynotes* by a writer such as "George Egerton," whom she classes as a new or "modern" female type (although, in the private correspondence between Marholm and "George Egerton" that ensued, the latter would once again disavow the New Woman label).

But even as Marholm argues for her vision of women's power over men, she also presents a more sinister picture of heterosexual relations in action in the social world. Using "George Egerton's" work as her illustration, she describes how the supposed comedy of "difference" inevitably degenerates, under the institutionalized inequality of marriage, into something violent and sordid, culminating in physical danger to the "little" woman from the "big" man, as well as psychological alienation and frustration on both sides:

> The . . . shudder is the deepest vibration in Mrs. Egerton's book. What is the subject? . . . . in every story it is the same little woman with a difference, the same little woman who is always loved by a big, clumsy, comic man, who is now good and well-behaved, now wild, drunk, and brutal, who sometimes ill-treats her, sometimes fondles her, but never understands what it is that he ill-treats and fondles. (*Modern Women,* 65)

What had started with female laughter ends on a very different note—the despairing sound of the narrative voice that Marholm hears throughout "George Egerton's" second volume of stories, *Discords* (1894):

> The tone of bitter disappointment which pervades "Discords" is the expression of woman's disappointment in man. Man and man's love are not a joy to her, they are a torment. He is inconsiderate in his demands, brutal in his caresses, and unsympathetic with those sides of her nature which are not there for his satisfaction. He is no longer the great, comic animal of "Keynotes," whom the woman teases and plays with—he is a nightmare which smothers her during horrible nights, a hangman who tortures her body and soul during days and years for his pleasure; a despot who demands admiration, caresses, and devotion, while her every nerve quivers with an opposite emotion; a man born blind, whose clumsy fingers press

> the spot where the pain is, and when she moans, replies with coarse, unfeeling laughter, "Absurd nonsense!" (*Modern Women,* 86–7)

By the end of Marholm's discourse, the issue of laughter has come full circle. Once again, the laugh is reinstated as a characteristic of male privilege, as a symptom of masculine hatred of women, and as an instrument of female humiliation and entrapment, rather than of female liberation. Given the context of the social and legal realities of late-nineteenth-century marriage, the "comedy" of sexual relations remains, for Marholm, a questionable concept and the laughing woman herself a problematic figure. And indeed, the version of the New Woman that Marholm admires—the one whose voice she finds in *Discords* and interprets for more conservative women readers—is not prone to comic flights. On the contrary, this New Woman has an "intense and morbid consciousness of . . . [her own] ego" (*Modern Women,* 79), "delicate nerves" on which "the sand of time falls drop by drop" (83), and a "tired, worn . . . restless . . . bitter, [and] hopeless" mien (83). She is a character who has given up on satire as a strategy, and her former attempts to "tease . . . and play . . . with" men and to treat them as humorous subjects are revealed as dangerously naive errrors.

For Marholm, then, the ultimate usefulness of female laughter was greatly in doubt. The impulse, in which the author herself indulges, to view men as comical and to look down at them co-exists uneasily here with the recognition of masculine power within patriarchy as absolute and of male hostility toward women as irremediable. Contemporary readers would have been at a loss to decide what course of action Laura Marholm was recommending: whether to go on countering the ferocity of the "Women-Haters" by "making fun" of man for being "so different from women" (*Modern Women,* 64–5), as she claimed women had been doing all along in secret, or whether instead to acknowledge the futility of such efforts and to abandon them. The fact that Marholm did not believe in or support any organized feminist movement for social change meant that she could not proffer any way out of this deadlock—this vision of women first laughing at suitors and then finding themselves helpless, laughed at, and abused by their captors after marriage. She could only present the issue of laughter as a complex socio-sexual problem, bound up with the unequal status of women, to be solved by someone else.

II

Long before Freud published his findings about the links between comedy and aggression, women intellectuals of the late-nineteenth century were pressed by circumstances into discerning this connection. There was no doubt that women in general—and any discontented, self-assertive, and vocal ones who could be labelled New Women, in particular—were being subjected on a wide scale to what Alice Meynell called the "great immorality" of sexist ridicule and that an angry, belligerent misogyny was behind this. Agreement broke down, though, over the proper response in a such a climate. Did it help or hurt women, as a group or individually, to laugh back? If this question ran as a continuing preoccupation through the essays of female literary and social critics, such as Meynell and Marholm, it proved an even greater issue for women authors of fiction. Through fiction, whether itself comic or serious in tone, New Women writers could explore the ramifications of being a woman who laughs, by figuring the personal consequences of making jokes at the expense of patriarchy and weighing the ultimate effects of such gestures in terms of other women's lives.

The fate of the middle-class woman who applies a comic perspective to her dealings with men became the special province of Ella Hepworth Dixon, especially in her works of the early Nineties, such as "A Literary Lover" and *My Flirtations* (1892). Like her contemporary Ada Leverson, who also moved socially in Oscar Wilde's set (Dixon contributed several pieces, as well, to the *Woman's World,* the magazine that Wilde edited), Dixon valued the exercise of wit in others and excelled in it herself. But wit, for her, could not be a virtue in itself, detached from other moral and political considerations. She was also a New Woman, as would be clear with the publication of her novel of social protest, *The Story of a Modern Woman* (1894), in which her characters dared to hope for a time when women would be "united . . . [and] could lead the world" (Dixon, *Story,* 259). And as a feminist, she refused to view any comedy that touched upon gender relations as separable from the serious business of women's unequal status under patriarchy.

The potential of laughter, within this context of inequality, to do women more harm than good became the subject of one of her early short stories for the magazine the *Woman's World.* In "A Literary Lover" (1890), the female protagonist finds herself alone in the sitting-room occupied by her houseguest, a man with whom she is in love and from whom she anticipates receiving a proposal. He is a novelist who has gone away overnight to consult with his publisher. As she pauses "reverently . . . wrapt in a happy dream" (Dixon, "Literary," 641) before the stray sheets of a manuscript that he has left lying on a writing desk, her eyes alight first upon a "page . . . full of clever paradoxes written in a slightly precieux style, and then [upon] . . . a brilliant phrase, the phrase of a master-mind, which rent the veil of convention and laid bare a palpitating human soul" (641). Riveted, she moves on to a sheet of notes all ready to be incorporated into her guest's witty, satirical novel of contemporary life: "She read on and on, until a hard smile gathered at the corners of her mouth and her fingers clenched the fragile scrap of paper . . . . The notes, elaborate, searching, brutal in their frankness, were about a woman—and that woman was herself" (641).

Her reaction is an interesting one. Stung though she is by her recognition of "the cruelty, the cynicism" (641) involved in his leading her on for the sake of "using her as a painter uses a model, to copy and thrust aside" (641), she still pays him the compliment of attributing his behavior to the "egotism of the artist" (641), rather than to mere caddishness. What is more, she allows herself to register that "hard smile" which signals bitterness and rue, but which also serves as a kind of tribute to the power of his words to amuse, even when the amusement comes at her own expense. So strong is her own artistic sensibility—so much is she, too, the "literary lover" of the story's title—that she can acknowledge almost admiringly the "brutal fidelity" with which he has rendered "her foolish, half-tender speeches, her appealing looks, her innocent little subterfuges for seeing him alone" (641), while also feeling betrayed and exposed.

The course of action on which she settles in response is, in fact, a further indication of her literary temperament. Knowing that he "had only done a third of his book, and he would want to study her for a long time to come" (641), she decides to punish him by writing him out of her own history, long before he has finished with her for his story. As she says to herself, employing the language of a novelist ridding herself of an unsuccessful fictional creation: "It was he who should be blotted out of her life as if he had never existed" (641).

Her method of accomplishing this end, moreover, shows that her sensibility is not only that of an artist, but of a comic artist in particular. She salves her damaged ego and restores herself to a position of superiority through the use of the smile. When her novelist-lover returns, she greets him both with the news that she must unexpectedly leave him and with "her prettiest smile" (641), an action that defies his analytic abilities: "He looked at her curiously, but her imperturbable smile baffled him" (641). Expecting her to announce that she has given up this summer-house in the country to settle in London, where he can have ready access to her, he is stunned to hear instead that she has made very different plans: "'I signed the lease last night for fourteen years. I am going to live here'" (641), she tells him "lightly" (641), capturing perfectly a comic tone in her delivery. She counters the sentimental melodrama of his final attempt to "press . . . her hand" (641) with a parting gesture of her own: "And then as the pony started off at a brisk trot, she turned and smiled back at him for the last time" (641). Her smile is a weapon that disarms him in many senses, depriving the novelist at once of an explanation of the situation, of a model for his work, and of his control over women.

Published at a historical moment when "Woman" served as the object of unprecedented satirical dissection and demolition by male authors, Dixon's story appears to present the kind of resistance to such abuse that twenty-first-century feminist theorists might applaud. The protagonist's method of re-erecting the boundaries that have been violated by her lover's literary caricature—her way of ensuring that he "at least, should never know the truth" (641) about her pain—would seem to be one endorsed by Regina Barreca, for instance, who asserts that "The strategic use of humor by a woman backed into a literal or figurative corner can have enormously positive results" (Barreca, *They Used to Call,* 95). In her 1991 work of feminist comic theory, *They Used to Call Me Snow White . . . But I Drifted,* which takes its title from a line penned by Mae West, Barreca argues throughout for the necessity of developing female "punchlines"—audacious comebacks to masculine hostility that disguises itself as humor. As Barreca delineates them, these "punchlines" depend, to paraphrase Oscar Wilde, far more on style than on sincerity. Speaking directly to her female audience, Barreca advises, "If and when you decide to use aggressive humor, you have to be sure to do it with finesse. It has to appear not to matter to you at all, otherwise it won't work. Like any joke, it depends on concealing the true feelings underneath" (Barreca, 97). Managed correctly, such behavior becomes a category of performance art. Indeed, the narrator of "A Literary Lover" points to just such a theatrical component, commenting upon the protagonist's success at carrying off the impenetrable smiles that function as her punchlines: "Most women are consummate actresses when their pride is at stake" (Dixon, "Literary," 641).

In current-day terms, the protagonist of "A Literary Lover" proves triumphant; Dixon's story records the victory of a character who first refashions herself through humor into an unreadable text, no longer available to exploitation by male authors, and then into a writer-performer who gets both the last word and the last laugh. Vengeance is hers, for as Barreca says, "Making a joke at the joker's expense is like making a cheat pay the tab when he thought he was going to be the one who got the free meal" (Barreca, 98). And the protagonist's actions would be exemplary in a world such as Barreca envisions in *They Used to Call Me Snow White . . .*, where only positive consequences follow from a good exit line:

> When a construction worker shouts at you as you walk down the street, "Hey, honey, I want to get into your pants," by all means shout back, "Nah, I got one asshole in there already." His pals will give him a hard time all day, and they might even applaud you . . . . (Barreca, *They Used to Call,* 98)

But for an end-of-the-nineteenth century feminist author such as Ella Hepworth Dixon, comedy represented neither so complete nor so simple a solution to women's dilemmas. (And the goal of getting a male audience to "applaud" could not have seemed an ideal strategy for countering the assumption that women's actions must be validated by men.) In "A Literary Lover," to be able to deliver the lines that frustrate her lover's purposes and buffet his vanity—"I signed the lease last night for fourteen years. I am going to live here" (Dixon, "Literary," 641)—the protagonist herself must pay a fearful price. Victory over her opponent comes at the cost of a self-imposed banishment to South Devonshire, far from the "artistic and intellectual set" (638) in London with which she feels most at home. The satisfaction produced by one minute of smiling revenge weighs against the sacrifice to be endured through fourteen solitary years ahead. Only thirty-six years old at the end of the narrative, she dooms herself to spend the prime of her creative and sexual life "stitching her . . . thoughts into the tea-cloth she was embroidering" (639). The choice that she had framed so drolly only days before, in hopes of gently prodding her lover on to a proposal—"I must settle what is to become of me—if I am to be a civilised being again, and live in London, or if it would be better for me to stay in the country, and end my days in a sober and sensible manner—'planting cabbages'" (640)—has in fact become the augury of her grim fate.

Women's comedy here is indistinguishable from women's tragedy, for the laughter leads to no transformation of the oppressive circumstances. Though the exercise of wit may have provided temporary relief from pain—and, thus, allowed her to survive the immediate situtation—it has done nothing either to increase the protagonist's own options by helping her to imagine and so to realize better ways of living or, on the other hand, to create new options for the female audience that exists beyond the text. To be the comic victor in this situation, Dixon's narrative appears to suggest, does not mean that one has escaped victimization; if anything, the attempted one-upping has further limited the protagonist's prospects and opportunities. Reacting to the masculine author who manipulates women and takes them "lightly" by giving him a taste of his own medicine still leaves the woman of 1890 with only a bitter pill to swallow herself. Indeed, if her "literary lover" were to observe the boredom and isolation of the retirement into which his actions have driven her, it is he who might have the last laugh.

In her first book-length volume, Ella Hepworth Dixon would return both to the subject of gender and laughter and to her own doubts about the lasting benefits for women of the comic perspective, pursuing more fully some of the questions raised by "A Literary Lover." Unlike the earlier story, however, which explored laughter thematically without being funny in itself, *My Flirtations,* published by Dixon in 1892 under the pseudonym "Margaret Wynman," was certainly among the finest surviving examples of turn-of-the-century feminist comedy.

Each of the chapters records the victory of the first-person narrator over one of the men whom she classifies as a past "flirtation," as she exposes to the readers' gaze his particular brand of narcissism, deceitfulness, greed, dullness, or condescension toward women. Yet the pattern established in Dixon's earlier story, "A Literary Lover," also proves paradigmatic here. Even as the narrator subjects one of these cold-hearted wooers to the lash of her laughter, the joke also recoils upon her; for to devote to these unsavory social types her time and attention—though it may be for the limited purpose of studying and reproducing their manners—necessarily involves her in their schemes, enables them to use her, and makes any more woman-centered sorts of activities impossible. (What such activities might include becomes clearer in Dixon's non-comic novel of 1894, *The Story of a Modern Woman,* where women assist and support one another.) Paradoxically, the focus upon producing comic subversion locks the protagonist into the masculine status quo.

The protagonist of *My Flirtations* is, like her father the Royal Academician, a painter of portraits, whose medium, however, is the comic prose sketch and whose studio is the family sitting-room. "We live in a nest of artists," she announces at the start (Dixon, *Flirtations,* 3), and the stories that follow attest to her own narrative art. But having men "sit" for her work is not the remote, detached activity that her father enjoys, nor is it a profession that pays. On the contrary, the pursuit of her "studies" is both a response to the pain that these suitors have caused her—a way of criticizing these types who prey upon unmarried, upper-middle-class young women and of distancing herself from the injuries and humiliations they have inflicted—and, unfortunately, a source of further pain. The decade of the Nineties would see many female and male writers addressing uneasily, in their fiction, the question of the proper relations between artists and those who serve as the inspiration for their material—indeed, between literature and social life in general (see Stetz, "Life's 'Half-Profits'"). In *My Flirtations,* the necessary dependence of comic art upon actual experience proves to have unhappy consequences for the author-figure. To get close enough to these "flirtations" in order to be able to capture their mannerisms and to skewer their affectations, as well as to be offended enough by their conduct to want to strike back through comedy, the narrator must enter their sphere and allow them to enter hers. It is an interpenetration that carries with it both emotional and social risks, though mainly for the woman.

Unlike the male "literary lover" of Dixon's earlier story, the woman author does not have the luxury of discarding her models when they have served her purpose or of remaining aloof from the entanglements of courtship, marriage, and domesticity. Laughing at men offers no protection against becoming romantically involved with them and having one's heart broken; neither does it ensure a way of life any different from the conventional, unsatisfactory path for a middle-class Victorian woman. Though the narrator of *My Flirtations* may, in the midst of the Oxford idyll of Chapter Four, come upon a place where "there leaped and danced hundreds of tiny, nimble, gay-hearted frogs, only lately emerged from the tadpole state" and remark acidly to her young male companion, "'They are *so* like undergraduates!'" (Dixon, *Flirtations,* 43), she will still feel the impulse to consent, when this particular undergraduate proposes. In the end, it is not so much her comic perspective that saves her from this match, but her doubts about her own place in his grandiose and even terrifying political schemes:

> The imperial destinies of the English race was one of his hobbies, and he asked me to give up London and go to North-Western Canada, where he wanted to start a new community. Visions of Margaret Fuller and the "Blithedale Romance," of Laurence Oliphant and his self-sacrificing bride, were evoked to tempt me. But I knew—I still had sense enough to know—that it was not for me . . . . (46)

Yet, despite her awareness of his coldbloodedly racist and imperialistic obsessions—"the last time I heard from him he was in South Africa, and I gathered from his letter that he considered the amalgamation, by marriage, of the Boer race the duty of all English settlers" (47)—and of his chilling belief in subordinating women to his political aims, she confesses to "times when I am a little tired of the . . . puerile frivolity of London young men . . . when I would give worlds to see Frank stretched in my deck-chair, his grey eyes gazing into futurity . . ." (47). Indeed, the strength of her attachment and the price that she pays for getting close enough to Frank to study him reveal themselves in the rhetorical use of ellipses, which punctuate the comedy of the chapter like rows of sentimental teardrops. They appear, for instance, amid her self-justification for allowing him to court her:

> He used to write me odd little abrupt notes, asking if I cared to see him? What could I say? It is awkward to tell people that you don't wish to see them. Besides—besides, I did want to . . . . [author's ellipses] (45)

And again, after she has turned down his proposal (one that recalls for the reader the equally unappealing offer of marriage from St. John Rivers to Charlotte Brontë's heroine, Jane Eyre) and refused to be the helpmeet who will assist in achieving his colonial ambitions, the ellipses suggest unspoken sorrow:

> And long after he had gone I sat on in the cold dark room. One by one the lamps twinkled out all up the street, and a dreary piano-organ came and played some threadbare airs from a comic opera . . . . [author's ellipses] Christina was very nice to me when she found me sitting alone in the cold and the dark, for I think she knew I had been crying . . . . [author's ellipses] (46)

Here, reminding the audience of the potential for an alternative, humorous point-of-view upon these proceedings—even by framing this scene generically against the "threadbare airs from a comic opera"—still does not liberate the narrator from her suffering or liberate the reader from empathizing with her. Instead of undercutting the sentimentality, the presence of such comic juxtaposition actually intensifies it. As Amanda Prynne, the female lead of Noel Coward's 1930 play *Private Lives,* might have said, "Extraordinary how potent cheap music is" (Coward, 207). So, too, the "comic opera" merely heightens, not dispels, the pathos.

The inability of the comic perspective either to guarantee women's emotional and physical survival, or to open up new social vistas that promise an end to oppression, becomes the theme of the final chapter of *My Flirtations,* where the narrator succumbs to her culturally appointed destiny. Neither as a personal nor as a political solution, it seems, is comedy sufficient. Though the narrator may begin by laughing both at men and at the upper-middle-class ideal of marriage, she, too, will become ensnared by them. In fact, to observe them closely enough to be able to satirize them is already to fall within their net.

Chapter Thirteen opens with the following dialogue, in which the twenty-year-old narrator laughs along with her sister, Christina, over a stockbroker who has just paid fifteen hundred pounds for a painting by their father and thus bought his way into becoming one of the family's social acquaintances:

> "Christina," I said thoughtfully one day when we were alone, "you are a young woman of sense and observation. Did it not occur to you, when Mr. John Ford dined here last night that he had the *cachet,* the unmistakable appearance of a *husband?*"
>
> "What do you mean, Peggy? What ridiculous notions you always have. Why everybody knows that John Ford is not, and has never been, married."
>
> "Oh, that's nothing," I retorted; "I tell you he was born to be henpecked, and to have a carriage with fat horses, and never drive in it and to pay long, expensive milliners' bills. The man looks like a husband. Some men don't and never will; let them marry three times and they never look as he looks."
>
> "Well, he hasn't shown any indecent haste about taking a wife," said Christina. "He must be every day of fifty."
>
> "No," I said meditatively, "he is forty-six—*mettons* forty-six. He likes French cooking and Italian operas (dear old fossils like the *Trovatore* and the *Traviata*), he is slightly rotund, he will give his wife a great many diamonds, and he will probably want to live in Prince's Gate. Now, if I were to marry a stockbroker, I would never wear diamonds. It is so like the City to wear diamonds. As a mere matter of taste, I should have nothing but sapphires and pearls . . . . And I should draw the line at Prince's Gate."
>
> "As you have only seen the man twice in your whole existence, I don't think you need disturb yourself about the locality you will inhabit with him—just yet."
>
> "Christina, don't interrupt my day-dream. As a matter of fact, I should insist on Mayfair. Not Charles Street, it's too gloomy; nor South Audley Street, it's too noisy; but, say, Park Street, or one of those cosy little cross streets—a red house with a white door and copper fixings."
>
> "Brass would be more appropriate for you, my dear girl," said Christina, sententiously; and then the thing slipped from my memory . . . . (154-5)

The mocking tone of this introduction would seem to predict a course of events much like that of previous chapters, in which the narrator begins by making light of a wooer and of the way of life that he embodies and ends by evading his matrimonial designs upon her. Such is the pattern, for instance, of Chapter Six, which opens with these observations:

> The provincial young man has never possessed any attractions for me, and it is certain that, if I had not gone up North to stay with Daisy Drysdale, I should never have known so well such a striking specimen of the type as Dr. Styles. He was not a bad fellow, but he was naively pleased with himself and his belongings . . . [for] in the limited circle of country-town society a suitable young man is pursuaded with too much pertinacity and ardour to have any doubts in his own mind as to his personal desirability and manifold charms. (61)

And indeed, it is the narrator's London-bred social snobbery, as much as anything, that impels her later to elude Dr. Styles's grasp, when he offers her "A lifetime of high tea, suburban gossip, and provincial self-sufficiency, of rose-bedecked door panels, the novels of H. Rider Haggard, and 'The Love that will never Fade'" (73). But it is the consciousness that he has sought her out for snobbish motives of his own, because "he remembered father's pictures, and was much impressed, apparently, by the fact that he was talking to an Academician's daughter" (64), that also makes her want to expose his pretentions and self-love to the reader's eye. He has viewed the woman merely as a social prize, an object glamorized by its association with patriarchal accomplishment and success (a situation that Dixon, daughter of William Hepworth Dixon, the renowned editor of the *Athenaeum,* certainly experienced at first hand). To laugh at such a suitor, therefore, is poetic justice—a matter of turning the tables and reducing him to an object, as well.

Yet that is not what occurs in the concluding chapter of *My Flirtations*. Although the dialogue between the sisters sets up "Mr. John Ford" as another figure of fun and the image of a "City" marriage as a rather shabby exercise in acquisitiveness and material display, the narrative does not end with the protagonist once again revelling in the freedom of her unmarried state. On the contrary, she loses that freedom through one of her own jokes. Seated next to the rather taciturn John Ford, she finds the "the conversation . . . [does] not flourish" (158) until she draws him out about his interests: "And such is the adaptability of woman and the egoism of man that before we left the dinner-table Mr. Ford was convinced that I cared for these things also" (158). They move on to the subject of investments, the masculine sphere of finance and public life from which Victorian women of her social class are usually excluded and in which they are uninstructed:

> "Contangos," "debentures," "bears," "bulls" have always been words of strange fascination for me, probably because I am totally ignorant of everything that goes on in the City. It came over me like madness that I wanted to have a little gamble, and Mr. John Ford offered to give me a "straight tip," as he called it, about Patagonians. And I, who never possessed more than 1*l*. 10*s*. altogether during my whole life, felt quite dissipated and worldly and reckless as we discussed the "little flutter" which I was to undertake. (158–9)

But what to her, living in the private and property-less world of the "young lady," is a comic flight of fancy is to him the serious business of men's occupations. Several days later, she discovers to her horror that her dinner-table acquaintance has actually bought the five shares that she had mentioned in jest and has sent her a bill for them. As she exclaims in dismay to her sister, Christina:

> "I've got to pay 50*l*. during the next fortnight! Great heavens!" I gasped. "Why, I haven't got a penny in the world! I was only joking—"
>
> "An odd sort of joke, my dear child," said Christina drily. "Couldn't you have remembered that rather important fact before?" (160)

Her comic turn has put her in the businessman's power, and the joke is on her. When she confesses her poverty to him, he enjoys the roles of financial protector, worldly superior, and indulgent father-figure, and also gets the last laugh:

> John Ford laughed. "Well, I think I can manage to get rid of 'em for you. In fact, I know a chap who wants five more." To anyone not blinded by financial terror, the little subterfuge must have been palpable. As it was, I never saw it till long afterwards . . . . There has never been a moment's doubt, from that day, that we should get on. (162)

With his dominance secured, Mr. John Ford is also primed to appreciate her as an object ready for the erotic equivalent of a corporate takeover bid. And, of course, her descent from a position of strength and independence to one of clinging feminine weakness has made possible their union, which can now proceed according to conventional lines.

My Flirtations concludes with the protagonist's wedding preparations. Yet the tone of this final section emphasizes both the narrator's unease with this course of events and, most certainly, Ella Hepworth Dixon's own resistance to sending her fictional creation off to this seemingly inexorable and less-than-desirable fate. Marriage was the expected and usually the inevitable end of Victorian comedies (a convention to which Virginia Woolf would allude mockingly in the historical pageant scene of her 1941 comedy, *Between the Acts,* where the chorus of Victorian ladies and gentlemen sings anxiously, "O has Mr. Sibthorp a wife? O has Mr. Sibthorp a wife?" [Woolf, 197]). In their professional lives, middle-class New Women writers of the Nineties acceded to the fact that it was impossible to pursue careers in the literary world without appealing (in several senses of the word) to men—whether publishers' readers, editors, owners of publishing firms, reviewers, or consumers—even to the very men who were laughing at them for wanting such careers in the first place. So, too, in New Women's comedies, marrying off the heroine signified acceptance of the necessity to cooperate with and accommodate oneself to the dominant culture, despite its hostility to women's best interests. The authors who bowed to this requirement did not always do so cheerfully or without protest. Yet, as Sally Ledger notes in *The New Woman* (1997), "The inability to think beyond heterosexual marriage as the only available route [for the plot]. . . explains the pessimism of most New Woman novels which reach an impasse on the marriage question" (Ledger, 23).

When Dixon sends her narrator off to marriage in *My Flirtations,* the comic spirit that has pervaded the narrative earlier disappears. It is replaced instead by sinister, even morbid, suggestions; as Thomas Hardy would have his Mrs. Edelin observe only four years later in *Jude the Obscure,* it would appear that "'Weddings be funerals 'a b'lieve nowadays'" (Hardy, 479), at least for the brides involved. Amidst her prenuptial preparations, the narrator reports that "Everyone in the house is very nice to me just now . . . . Nobody contradicts me. It reminds me of once, long ago, when I was ill. And to be sure I am tired, very tired" (*Flirtations*, 162–3). If being engaged is likened to a sickness, then it is a condition with a grim prognosis. As the narrator says of the formalities surrounding the marriage settlements:

> There are those nervous interviews, too, with grinning, sporting-looking attorneys in Lincoln's Inn Fields, when perfectly incomprehensible documents without stops are read out to me, and I finally put my signature on a parchment, which makes one feel for all the world as if one were signing a death-warrant. (164–5)

Most ominous of all is the language of the book's closing scene, which sees the narrator carrying what appears at first to be her own coffin: "One foggy winter afternoon I toil upstairs to Christina's room, dragging after me, with the help of the maid, a long, brown, wooden box" (166). When pried open, this rather Gothic "box" proves to hold contents at once mysterious and awful:

> [We] bend curiously over the box as the maid lifts gingerly out a garment of shimmering white and silver from under a layer of tulle.
>
> Symbols of the Eternal Feminine, those lengths of glittering satin flaunt themselves over the sofa and along the floor, lighting up the dim little room with their sumptuous whiteness, while, like a June cloud, the foam of tulle floats for an instant in the winter dusk.
>
> It is my wedding gown. (167)

And thus ends the narrative of *My Flirtations,* using an image that combines allusions to shrouds and grave-clothes with reminders of the Victorian penchant in the visual arts, as well as in literature, for conflating middle-class women with angels (see Stetz, "Ella Hepworth Dixon," 103). For Dixon's heroine, it would seem that to marry is to become an angel by dying. There is scarcely more reason to hope that the narrator will be able to survive this marriage, whether psychically or physically, than that Rachel Vinrace can survive hers in Virginia Woolf's novel of 1915, *The Voyage Out*—a work that Ann Ardis has rightly linked with "various issues associated with the New Woman during the 1890s" (Ardis, 169).

Authors of the 1890s were still bound by narrative conventions that required marriage to be the "happy ending" for the plot of women's comedies, and particularly for those intended for publication as serials in mainstream, popular magazines directed at a general audience. (*My Flirtations* appeared first in the *Lady's Pictorial,* before being issued in book form by Chatto and Windus.) Ella Hepworth Dixon submitted to using marriage as the conclusion to her plot, but stripped this necessity of its "happy" pretense; instead, she riddled the ending with allusions to sickness and death. Yet the impossibility of avoiding the use of marriage as climax to the action suggests one of the problems attached to writing late-Victorian feminist comedy and turning to laughter as an answer to misogynistic and oppressive situations. Poking fun at the world of masculine ideologies and institutions from up-close and from the inside, by embroiling the "respectable" middle-class heroine in that world, meant that the author would have to build her plot toward the very union that ritualized female dependency and male dominance. Editors encouraged if not demanded it, as did reviewers. The conventions associated with comic structure were, seemingly, even more inflexible than those for other forms of fiction at the turn of the century, and they closed off imaginative possibilities beyond the text for readers, as well as possibilities for alternative resolutions to the fates of the characters. Perhaps for this reason, Dixon abandoned comedy entirely in her next New Woman novel, *The Story of a Modern Woman* (1894). There, she concluded the plot irresolutely, avoiding the closure of marriage; the middle-class female protagonist remains uncertain about her future and even her survival, but still independent and still struggling against the political tyranny of patriarchal institutions, as well as the emotional tyranny of the men in her life.

For those New Women writers, however, who were not ready to give up on comedy, there were ways of fulfilling the demand for a wedding at the end of the narrative, yet continuing to debunk the myth that heterosexual romance guaranteed happiness for women or that marriage was always the most desirable outcome for a plot. E. [Edith] Nesbit, for instance, used the discordant commentaries of her shrewd and cynical female narrators in several of the stories from *In Homespun* (1896) as antiphonal voices, working against the sentimentality of the marriage plots. They were there to remind readers instead that money, class, and patriarchal power were the forces that usually determined both the structure of heterosexual relationships and their outcomes.

Nesbit, a committed socialist, was unusual among New Women writers in drawing her narrators from among the working-classes and lower-middle-classes. Though Amelia A. Rutledge may claim that "there was little that was original in her adult fiction," placing such characters in the foreground of her fiction, instead of relegating them to the status of mere foils for rebellious middle-class heroines, was indeed an innovative decision (Rutledge, 223). Nesbit's protagonists were inhabitants of small country towns and villages; they were ill-educated, yet articulate, figures who recognized that they had been tethered by economic circumstances, but who refused to become entrapped, as well, by the romantic ideology that bound other women. They were not "New Women" according to definitions that Ann Ardis developed in the now-classic study, *New Women, New Novels: Feminism and Early Modernism* (1990)—that is, they did not put female relationships first and "sustain each other as they pursue[d] ambitions that, for whatever reason, the men in their lives . . . [could not or would] not endorse" (Ardis, 134); neither were they participants in or sympathizers with any organized feminist movement.

On the contrary, Nesbit's working-class characters saw other women—even their closest female relations—who did buy into myths of romantic love both as fools and as obstacles to their own survival, toward whom they could not afford to be indulgent. But they were New Women nonetheless, in approaching political institutions such as marriage and domesticity with suspicion and in struggling to keep free of illusions that could leave them vulnerable to masculine exploitation or social control.

The comic narrator-protagonist, for example, of Nesbit's "Acting for the Best," one of the short stories from the 1896 volume *In Homespun,* begins with the proposition that "people [i.e., women] who talk that kind of nonsense about marrying for love and the like" (Nesbit, 104) are self-deluders:

> For my part I don't know what they mean, and I don't believe they know it themselves. It's only a sort of fashion of talking. I never could see what there was to like in one young man more than another, only, of course, you might favour some more than others if they was better to do. (Nesbit, *In Homespun,* 104)

Her own situation has made her conscious of the financially dependent position of women, for she is an orphan, living on the farm of her uncle along with his daughter, her cousin Mattie. The narrative's action concerns the ensuing events when Mattie's sweetheart, whom the uncle had not considered a suitable prospect three years earlier, returns from America—"assisted emigration," as the narrator explains tartly (106). Having made his fortune, he sends word that "'I mean to take a wife back with me, Mattie, for I have done well, and can afford to keep one in better style than your father kept his. Will you be her, dear?'" (109)—phrasing which suggests that the category of "wife" will take precedence over the individual occupant of it. Mattie, who has clung to her affection for Jack with the tenacity of an Amelia Sedley pining for the unworthy George Osborne of Thackeray's *Vanity Fair,* rushes off to meet him on the one day when he will be passing through the village. But the narrator intervenes, locking Mattie in the local church and showing up in her place for the rendezvous with Jack:

> When I locked her in I only meant to have a sort of joke—at least, I think so,—but when I come close up to him and saw how well off he looked, and the diamond ring on his fingers . . . I thought to myself—. . . .
>
> If she didn't care for money why should she have it, when there was plenty that did? And if love in a cottage was what she wanted, and kisses

> and foolishness out of poetry-books, I suppose one man's pretty much as good as another for that sort of thing. (111)

Jack accepts with total credulity both her improbable account of Mattie's change of heart and the fiction that she herself "has been thinking of him steady and faithful these three years"—a tale that she accompanies with what anyone less full of himself would recognize as an outrageously transparent bit of sentimental theatricalism. The signifiers of feminine submission that heterosexual romance demands are, as the narrator discerns, merely a set of gestures—a *performance.* As the narrator says, "I just lifted my eyes up and looked at him, and dropped them. I've always practised looking like what I meant, or what I wanted people to think I meant—sort of matching your looks and words, like you match ribbon and a bit of stuff" (118). The nearly successful plot of this writer-performer, who "acts" for her own "best," is spoiled, however, when Mattie frantically rings the church bells, bringing out the whole village to free her and reunite her with Jack. And with his new wealth enabling him, as he himself puts it, "'to keep my little girl as she should be kept'" (123), Jack even wins over Mattie's father, who affirms that his former objections were purely "'for your own good and hers'" (124).

In the hands of an author with a different position on gender politics, this would have constituted the "happy ending" of a romantic comedy—the thwarting of the female villain who has schemed to keep a pair of true lovers apart. Within such a traditional framework, the audience would have been invited to see the thoroughly serious "joke" that the narrator had tried to play upon Mattie and Jack as having turned into an actual joke that recoils only upon the narrator herself. Readers would have laughed only at her and at her discomfiture, while cheering on the marriage that she had opposed. But E. Nesbit—who, according to her biographer Julia Briggs, befriended and admired Eleanor Marx-Aveling, Charlotte Wilson, Olive Schreiner, Charlotte Perkins Gilman, and other New Women of the day (Briggs, xviii) and who consciously violated social norms and taboos in her own untraditional marriage to Hubert Bland—used the comic structure of the story to ridicule the fictions of heterosexual romance, not to mock the narrator-protagonist. The closing image of the supposedly devoted lovers going off together positions itself ironically against the readers' knowledge of how easily the narrator was able to rewrite that scenario and to insert herself in Mattie's place. Barely minutes before leaving with his arm around Mattie, Jack had sealed with an energetic kiss his pledge to marry the narrator instead. Given these circumstances, the final pairing reveals itself as an arbitrary, businesslike, and unglamorous arrangement—one that merely suits the convenience of a bridegroom, who views brides as interchangeable and replaceable parts.

As part of her anti-romantic strategy, Nesbit leads the audience to laugh disapprovingly at the so-called hero of this romance, even more than at the narrator who would disrupt it. He is an unpleasant character who damns his beloved as "Wicked, heartless" and as a "little witch," when it appears that she has given him up, but who sees no faithlessness in his own readiness to marry the narrator in her stead that very day. The quite suggestively named "Jack Halibut" thus proves himself rather a cold fish. Any reader (except for guileless Cousin Mattie) of his original letter of proposal would have discerned that his interest lay merely in acquiring a wife as a kind of bourgeois ornament, to go along with his new social position abroad. Indeed, he almost boasts of this to the narrator, while making his second proposal: "'Look here, I'm well off. I'm going to Liverpool to-night, and back to America next week. I want to take a wife with me . . . . I marries my wife, and I takes her right away.'" (Nesbit, 118–19). His concept of "a wife" is a generic one, into which any English woman of a slightly higher social status might fit. Though he assumes the pose of an injured lover, when he thinks that Mattie has changed her mind after his three years of silence, his actual fidelity to the romantic ideal is no greater than that of the narrator. "Love" is not an emotion that he feels himself, but merely what any virtuous woman is expected to *perform* for him, as proof of her virtue. Astoundingly enough, he finds nothing remarkable about the assertion of someone whom he scarcely knows that she would have loved him "steady and faithful" in secret for years.

Under the circumstances, the narrator's conduct in locking up her cousin and taking her place serves as an inspired jest with a strong feminist undercurrent. Although the characters within Nesbit's short story may be blind to its implications, contemporary readers would have realized that this "joke" has exposed the masculine self-conceit, hypocrisy, bullying, social ambition, and economic one-upmanship that can conceal themselves behind the fabric of the late-Victorian marriage system. In the name of romance, hapless women such as Mattie are worshipped or damned, courted or pushed aside at will by those who wish to acquire them from their fathers' households, uproot them, and re-install them as trophies in their own. As the story ends, marriage continues to be an institution that benefits men and that remains part of their privilege to bestow or to withhold, whether as suitors or as fathers. Only the narrator has registered any protest against these conditions, by attempting to rewrite the romantic fiction as a comic fiction and to wrest the power over female fate away from Jack and from her uncle. Yet that creative effort on the part of the narrator proves futile, helping neither herself nor Cousin Mattie to get what these women deserve. Mattie's final gesture of reconciliation—"'Oh, never mind all that now, Jack,' she says, with arms round his neck. 'What does it matter about a silly joke now that I have got you, and it's all right betwixt us?'" (123)—assumes a comic irony that shades into pathos. It is Jack, not she, who is in charge—who has "got" his bride, to "takes [sic] her right away" (119) with him abroad as he chooses. Meanwhile, the capricious and selfish behavior that he has just exhibited suggests to the audience that nothing really has been "all right betwixt" them in the past or will be so in future.

In the end, Mattie has been handed from her domineering father to her domineering husband, exchanging one subordinate role for another, while the narrator remains trapped in economic dependency in her uncle's house. Clearly, in Nesbit's "Acting for the Best," the woman's joke has no immediate power either to alter the course of individual fates or to reform the unsatisfactory social and political arrangements that lie behind these. All that this joke can achieve is the enlightenment of the reader. For E. Nesbit, that may have been enough to justify the writing of ironic feminist comedy. Her subsequent abandonment, however, of fiction for adult consumption and her immersion in children's literature and fantasy genres suggests otherwise. As Amelia A. Rutledge puts it, "The fairy tale offered Nesbit a socially acceptable (and profitable) venue for publication and a flexible structure that would admit of variations in plot and even departures from convention . . . . (Rutledge, 227). Like many other New Women writers, E. Nesbit appears to have become frustrated with the limited possibilities for change offered by laughter—at least in fiction directed at adults—and to have gone in search of other modes and other audiences. In her case, this meant seeking out audiences who were at an earlier and more impressionable stage of life, where there was more hope of exercising influence upon them and impelling them to remake the world beyond the text.

III

Despite the ambivalence toward laughter demonstrated by numerous feminists and feminist-sympathizers throughout the Nineties, men continued to fear attack from that direction, even as they launched their own satirical assaults upon those who refused to behave as middle-class domestic angels. And, paradoxically, the more these masculine critics insisted that New Women had no sense of humor, the more they appeared to dread the spectre of her ridicule. Evidently, it seemed to them impossible that a New Woman would have any agenda but the annihilation of men, or that she might entertain moral objections to using the weapons that had been turned against her—or, in fact, that she might judge such masculine instruments to be shoddy and ineffective ones for achieving her own, quite different, goals. If she were heard to be laughing, then it would assuredly be in the same way that they had laughed at her. The repeated representations, in both journalistic writing and cartooning alike, of New Women as inevitably and uniformly a set of "mannish, over-educated, humourless bores"—to use Sally Ledger's description (Ledger, 26)—became a way of denying the emergence of the witty and possibly seductive feminists and feminist texts that men feared, as well as a means of undercutting the influence of those that had already appeared.

Ella D'Arcy, a writer who moved at the margins of New Womanhood, made the paranoid and potentially lethal pursuit of the bogey of the Laughing Feminist the subject of an 1895 short story. For "The Pleasure-Pilgrim," which appeared first in the *Yellow Book* (where D'Arcy was employed as sub-editor) and then in the Bodley Head volume *Monochromes,* D'Arcy borrowed much of her framework from Henry James's 1878 novella, *Daisy Miller.* Her narrative resembled James's, in its use of the theme of misapprehension across cultures and genders. But the result was an even darker *Daisy Miller,* reconceived through the lens of the masculine anxiety and murderous misogyny that infected British intellectual circles of the 1890s. Though D'Arcy's heroine warns, "'I think men gossip a great deal more than women . . . and they don't understand things either. They try to make all life suit their own pre-conceived theories'" (D'Arcy, 150), she herself gets appropriated by the men around her and labelled a laughing Medusa-figure—a constricting process of patriarchal definition from which there is no escape, except at the price of her life.

Campbell, D'Arcy's male protagonist, is a young English novelist who has come back to Germany and to a castle-turned-guesthouse for a summer of writing. Travelling alone, he appears neither to have formed nor sought any attachments to individual women, preferring only a distant and generalized attitude of reverence toward "the sex" as a category: "He had a high ideal of Woman, an immense respect for her; he could not endure to hear her belittled, even in jest" (D'Arcy, 142). Accompanying this abstract esteem of Woman (with a capital "W," of course) is a deep suspicion of female power that makes him suppress his own erotic desires:

> He had a special fear of being fooled. For beneath a somewhat supercilious exterior, the dominant note of his character was timidity, distrust of his own merits; and he knew . . . if he were . . . to get to care very much for a woman . . . he would lose himself completely, be at her mercy absolutely. (151)

His only apparent connection with others, indeed, is his relationship with a fellow-lodger, Mayne, a married man with whom he has enjoyed "good talks . . . late at night, before the great fire in the hall, after the rest of the household had gone to bed" (131). The homoerotic undercurrents to this intimacy, as well as the intellectual competitiveness and heterosexual rivalry with Campbell and with other men that Mayne displays, become important elements in the triangulated drama that follows.

Trouble ensues with Campbell's introduction to another guest already in residence, Lulie Thayer, a rich young woman from Detroit, Michigan, who is travelling with a female companion. The companion, Nannie Dodge, repels him from the start—not so much because her features strike him as "sallow" and "nondescript" (134), but because she arouses his lingering fear of being mocked and diminished by women. A professional writer, used to shielding himself behind the power of the masculine gaze, he detects the

> immense amount of humorous meaning which lurked in her gaze. When her pale prominent eyes met Campbell's, it seemed to the young man that they were full of eagerness to add something at his expense to the stores of information they had already garnered up. They chilled him with misgivings . . . . (134–5)

In Lulie Thayer, however, he believes that he discerns only "a simple child-like manner that was charming" (137). Better still, her red hair, "strange little face," and "queer eyes" gradually register upon him "as being pretty—in a peculiar way":

> He felt an immense accession of interest in her. It seemed to him that he was the discoverer of her possibilities. He did not doubt that the rest of the world called her plain; or at least odd-looking . . . . Her charm was something subtle, out-of-the-common, in defiance of all known rules of beauty.

> Campbell saw the superiority in himself for recognizing it, for formulating it; and he was not displeased to be aware that it would always remain caviare to the multitude. (137–8)

Afterwards, like many a nineteenth-century British imperial traveller who was sure that he had come upon unexplored territory, Campbell is eager to return to the old world that he knows and to boast of his exclusive claim upon this new one—particularly to his fellow man, who can understand the power that being the first to *penetrate* the feminine will give him:

> And, full of his great discovery, he felt he must confide it to Mayne, at least. "Do you know," he went on, "*she* is really very pretty too? I didn't think so at first, but after a bit I discovered that she is positively quite pretty—in an odd sort of way." (141)

He is, therefore, disappointed to learn that he is not the first to make this "great discovery" and that his announcement has merely opened him up to ridicule by another man; for if he fears being "fooled" by women, he dreads nearly as much looking foolish to other men:

> Mayne laughed again. "Pretty, pretty!" he echoed in derision. "Why, *lieber Gott im Himmel,* where are your eyes? Pretty! The girl is beautiful, gorgeously beautiful; every trait, every tint, is in complete, in absolute harmony with the whole." (141)

The respective aesthetic tributes they pay to Lulie's features take on a competitive dimension (see Stetz, "Debating Aestheticism," 37–9), as Mayne, the cultivated amateur, goes the professional writer one better in praising her:

> "You speak of Miss Thayer's hair as red . . . . [But] what a red it is! It looks as though it had been steeped in red wine."
>
> "Ah, what a good description," said Campbell appreciatively. "That's just it—steeped in red wine." (141)

The image, alas, proves a prophetic one, suggesting both men's willingness to see the beauty of a woman's face surrounded by that other red-wine-like agent—blood.

If Campbell is dismayed to find that he cannot hold first claim to Lulie as a new piece of visual property (Stetz, "Debating Aestheticism," 37–9), he is horrified to hear Mayne assert that this territory may not be virgin in other respects. Lulie Thayer, or so Mayne insists, is "'the most egregious little flirt I've ever met'" (142), someone who "'makes love—desperate love, mind you—to every man she meets'" (146), in order to have the fun of drawing back and mocking him. What is more, "'during a brief season, I must tell you, my young lady had the caprice to show attentions to your humble servant'" (145), though his own lack of responsiveness as a married man allegedly drove her into the arms of another guest. Mayne says,

> "Providence, taking pity on Miss Thayer's forced inactivity, sent along March, a young fellow reading for the army, with whom she had great doings. She fooled him to the top of his bent; sat on his knee, gave him a lock of her hair . . . and got him to offer her marriage. Then she turned round and laughed in his face, and took up with a Dr[.] Weber, a cousin of the Baron's, under the other man's very eyes." (145–6)

Neither Campbell nor the reader ever observes such proceedings at first-hand in the course of the story. As proof, there is only the tradition of masculine authority that lies behind the word of Mayne, who offers as his one piece of concrete evidence Lulie's alpenstock. Mayne chooses to read this object as a text and to interpret its narrative as that of a comic-epic—a record, in phallic shape, of a war upon men:

> [It] was decorated with a long succession of names, which, ribbon-like, were twisted round and round it, carved in the wood.
>
> "Read them," insisted Mayne, putting the stick in Campbell's hands . . . .
>
> "[They're] the names of the men she has fooled. And there's room for more; there's still a good deal of space, as you see. There's room for yours." (146)

Again and again, Mayne succeeds in crushing Campbell's potential desire for Lulie by exciting his friend's deepest anxieties about being made to look ridiculous: "'I can see she means to add you to her ninety-and-nine other spoils; I saw it from the way she looked at you at dinner,'" he cautions (142). Although his own obsessive conduct would seem to indicate a complex web of jealousies and frustrations, some of them homoerotic, he accuses Lulie of being driven by so-called psychosexual abnormalities—perversity, frigidity, and quasi-lesbian attachments among them. The misogynist tirade into which he launches, by way of "explaining" Lulie, is a remarkable summary of many of the criticisms that Ella D'Arcy would have heard levelled against herself and other female contemporaries, both in literature and in life:

"I don't think, mind you," he said, "that she is a bit interested herself in the men she flirts with. I don't think she gets any of the usual sensations from it, you know. My theory is, she does it for mere devilry, for a laugh. Or, and this is another theory, she is actuated by some idea of retribution. Perhaps some woman she was fond of—her mother even—who knows?—was badly treated at the hands of a man. Perhaps this girl has constituted herself the Nemesis for her sex, and goes about seeing how many masculine hearts she can break, by way of revenge. Or can it be that she is simply the newest development of the New Woman—she who in England preaches and bores you, and in America practises and pleases? Yes, I believe she's the American edition, and so new that she hasn't yet found her way into fiction. She's the pioneer of the army coming out of the West, that's going to destroy the existing scheme of things, and rebuild it nearer to the heart's desire." (147)

Primed by Mayne to "read" Lulie as a text with this one particular signification—as a walking satire, a living-and-breathing New Woman comedy that uses the romance plot punitively, to make fun of men—Campbell rudely and self-protectively fends off first her offers of friendship and then her professions of love. The more he resists, however, the more enamored she appears to grow. But under the tutelage of Mayne—who, in his "latest theory about our young friend," accuses her of being "an actress, a born comedienne" (157) and thus of *performing* desire—Campbell remains convinced that she is merely laughing at him. He decides, moreover, that he must beat her to the punchline, defusing her power by laughing at her instead:

For she made him all sorts of silent advances, speaking with her eyes, her sad little mouth, her beseeching attitude . . . .

And when he began to utter evasive banalities, she stopped him with an imploring "Ah, don't! I love you. You know I love you. I love you so much I can't bear you to put me off with mere phrases."

Campbell admired the well-simulated passion in her voice, remembered Mayne's prediction, and laughed aloud.

"Oh, you may laugh," she said, "but I'm serious. I love you, I love you with my whole soul." (153)

Nannie Dodge, her companion, backs up this claim, countering Campbell's sarcastic dismissal of Lulie as having "'cried "Wolf" too often before to expect to be believed now.'" She says instead, "'But . . . the wolf did really come at last, you know . . . We've all made mistakes in our lives, haven't we? But that's no reason for not being right at last'" (157). Campbell's fear of falling prey to the mockery of the New Woman, however, and thus of losing control over the narrative of their relations, gives the victory to Mayne, who has "set himself . . . determinedly to spoil her game" (164). When Lulie, after whiling away an hour by shooting at targets, makes another of her ardent declarations of love, Campbell turns upon her, blasting the American with the puritanically English judgment of a rigid and misogynistic ideology of gender. He says,

> "Why, if you really loved me, really loved any man—if you had any conception of what the passion of love is, how beautiful, how fine, how sacred—the mere idea that you could not come to your lover fresh, pure, untouched, as a young girl should—that you had been handled, fondled, and God knows what besides, by this man and the other—would fill you with such horror for yourself, with such supreme disgust—you would feel yourself so unworthy, so polluted . . . that . . . that . . . by God! you would take up that pistol there, and blow your brains out!" [author's ellipses] (173)

Her response is a fascinatingly ambiguous one: "'And suppose I were to,' she asked lightly, 'would you believe me then?'" (173). D'Arcy deliberately leaves open multiple ways of reading the adverb "lightly." Is it proof of Lulie's satirical bent and thus of the fact that she is indeed toying with Campbell and laughing at him? Is it evidence of the depth of her obsession with Campbell and of the despair that has overcome her in the face of his rejection, making her indifferent to her own survival? Or is it the sign of her attempt to preserve her dignity in the face of his verbal assault—an effort to respond "lightly," as the heroine of Dixon's "A Literary Lover" did when psychologically injured—by assuming a facetious tone to cover her pain? Is it, indeed, a final and futile effort to discover a way to survive through the use of comedy? No narrative authority intervenes to settle this for the reader and thus to determine Lulie's "meaning."

Unlike Ella D'Arcy, the New Woman author who prefers to leave these complex questions of motivation unresolved and irresolvable through narrative, Campbell, the male novelist-figure within the story, must fix upon a single reading for the woman's action. In this case, he relies upon the interpretation that Mayne, the story's other masculine authority, has already supplied. In Mayne's eyes, Lulie is simply the man-hating "comedienne." Thus, even as Lulie picks up the gun and points it at herself, Campbell reads in her appearance a "little tragic air, which seemed to him so like a smile disguised" (173), the secret smile that he has always dreaded, sure that it must be at his expense. And in the seconds after she has fired the fatal shot into her body, he still chooses to believe that mere mockery of him is at play and to view her apprehensively as the one who may have control of the situation, right up until the moment of her death:

> There came a sudden, sharp crack, a tiny smoke film. She stood an instant swaying slightly, smiling certainly, distinctly outlined against the background of rain-washed window, of gray falling rain, the top of her head cutting in two the Rittenhausen escutcheon. Then all at once there was nothing at all between him and the window . . . but a motionless heap of plush and lace, and fallen wine-red hair, lay at his feet upon the floor. (173)

Between them, Campbell and Mayne, prompted by their fear of erotic ridicule at the hands of this supposed New Woman, have driven Lulie into a corner—the one constructed for the "fallen"—from which there is no escape, except through death. Her hair is, at last, steeped in the red wine of her own blood, as they have seemingly both predicted and desired.

But the final joke of the narrative is on Campbell and also on those of D'Arcy's masculine readers who would have been equally anxious about contemporary women's unconventional behavior and equally desperate to have female conduct and motives "explained," once and for all, by literary texts—especially, the texts produced by New Women themselves. For the heroine, in fact, has eluded those who would define her. In an ending that is wonderfully innovative for late-Victorian realist fiction, D'Arcy withholds judgments or pronouncements by any central narrative authority and concludes instead merely with the competing voices of two of the story's fictional characters. In the opinion of Nannie Dodge, Lulie was "'the most loving girl in the world'"; because she was "'tremendously, terribly in love'" with Campbell, "'when she found that you wouldn't care about her, she didn't want to live any more,'" Nannie tells him (174). Yet Mayne is just as adamant in insisting upon the contrary, saying,

> "But, believe me, she was only fooling with you . . . . [Lulie's suicide] was just her histrionic sense of the fitness of things. The role she had played so long and so well now demanded a sensational finale in the centre of the stage . . . . She was the most consummate little actress I ever met." (175)

Both readings have equal weight and validity, and Campbell, who hopes that the two interpreters might "have resolved his doubts one way or the other" (174), remains forever tormented by his inability to choose between them.

Here, Ella D'Arcy, the New Woman writer, does indeed have the last laugh. Yet once again, any sense of triumph must be tempered by the reader's knowledge of the price that triumph exacts. In the context of late-Victorian gender inequalities, such a comic victory can be achieved only through the suffering and self-destruction of the story's female protagonist. Without a movement toward tangible social change to back it up, the laugh of the New Woman proves merely to be a smile before dying.

IV

And die the New Woman did—or, at least, so it seemed. By the end of the 1890s, with their novelty no longer a selling point to outweigh the masculine resistance and backlash that they had provoked, New Women authors would experience growing difficulty in finding either publishers or audiences. Ella D'Arcy lapsed into relative silence, resurfacing only as the English translator of Andre Maurois's biography of Shelley. In later years, Ella Hepworth Dixon, like many of her female contemporaries who published little after the turn of the century, at least in the genre of prose fiction, disavowed the title of "New Woman" entirely. For her 1930 memoirs, *As I Knew Them,* she would even chronicle an occasion on which Edmund Gosse had referred to her as one and would remark, "Why I should have been so called I never knew, except that I had always been in favour of the Women's Franchise" (Dixon, *As I Knew Them,* 41).

If it became increasingly uncomfortable merely to be identified as a New Woman, it certainly proved impossible to go on laughing as one. Wounded and humiliated by the years they had spent as the butt of jokes, some literary survivors of the Nineties would even try to obliterate their psychic scars by going over to the enemy camp and turning against those who resembled their former selves. "George Egerton" (Mary Chavelita Dunne), for instance, the erstwhile author of *Keynotes, Discords*, and other fiction that had led Laura Marholm to hail her as a voice of rebellion against male oppression, would write a thoroughly unfunny, reactionary stage comedy in 1911 called *The Backsliders,* mocking those women who protested against the social order, put careers before domesticity, or dared to attempt to express themselves through writing and publishing.

But were the rumors of the New Woman's death exaggerations, or perhaps anti-feminist wishful thinking? In recent years, feminist revisionist literary historians such as Ann Ardis, Marianne DeKoven, and Lynn Pykett, who have reconsidered late-Victorian and turn-of-the-century fiction, have argued convincingly that the impress of the New Woman—at least in the literary sphere—never really disappeared. Instead, the "rebellious structures" of narrative fiction, as Gerd Bjørhovde has labelled them, that were engendered by New Women authors as the vehicles for rebellious political ideologies provided the direction for subsequent twentieth-century developments in form and content. In effect, they inaugurated modernist and even post-modernist experimentalism. Indeed, the formal innovations of a text such as Ella D'Arcy's short story, "The Pleasure-Pilgrim," with its dual-voiced and its closure-resistant ending, were immense and certainly influential.

What did the laugh of the New Woman, in particular, leave as its legacy? Perhaps the chief contribution of late-Victorian feminist humorists was in the area of attitudes, rather than of form. Paradoxically, they did most for comedy by alerting their readers to its limitations and by reminding audiences not to ask the impossible of it. New Women writers showed themselves quite capable of being funny. When, therefore, they chose to mute or temper their ridicule, or to write about the problems surrounding the deployment of laughter, instead of merely revelling in laughter itself, they did so with good cause. Partly, they were led to their distrust of laughter by an awareness of the moral complexities that ringed round the act of targeting an enemy for ridicule. But doubts about the effectiveness of laughter as a concrete political strategy proved an even more important factor. Focused as the New Women were on the world outside of the literary text and conscious as they were of the specific social and economic conditions of the actual women surrounding them (women, moroever, of many classes, including those who were not consumers of printed books), they hesitated to put all their faith and energies into an activity that offered only limited potential for creating change. Time would show them to be right, moreover, as members of the next generation of feminists, women writers of the British Suffrage movement, would find it easy to make audiences laugh, with comic plays such as *How the Vote Was Won* (1909), by Cicely Hamilton and "Christopher St[.] John" (Christabel Marshall), but difficult to move those audiences from laughter to action.

New Women of the 1890s had no illusions about the power of their comic literature alone to bring down the old order or to inaugurate a new one. The warning that Audre Lorde would issue to feminists in a different context almost one hundred years later—"For the master's tools will never dismantle the master's house. They may allow us temporarily to beat him at his own game, but they will never enable us to bring about genuine change" (Lorde, 99)—was one that they already knew to be true and tried to live by.

Today, at a time when academic feminist culture seems inclined to overvalue the role of laughter as a "subversive" force in art and politics, turning to it reverently, whether as a corrective or as a guide, and holding up women comics from Mae West to Roseanne to Ellen DeGeneres to Dawn French and Jennifer Saunders as heroes, it might be wise to remember the skepticism of the New Women one hundred years ago. Even as they laughed, they recognized that satire is no substitute for political solidarity and that poking fun at patriarchy cannot do the work of organized action.

CHAPTER TWO

Rebecca West's "Elegy": Women's Laughter and Loss

> How awkward that I should have met you when I am behaving so badly, walking along the street shrieking with laughter! But you will understand that I can't help laughing when I tell you what has happened to-day. It's funny, so funny! You really must excuse me. But listen! Listen! I want you to hear it. You see, it is about Mother. ("Elegy," 183)

So begins Rebecca West's short story from 1929, called "Elegy." In retrospect, the eagerness of the narrator to reach out to that unidentified "you" and to tell her tale to the audience rings with a special irony, for this is a story which has, in effect, remained entirely unheard—lost to the world since it was published in 1929. Curiously enough, not even the most dedicated of West's readers appear to have realized that it was missing. But then, they would have had to stumble upon it by accident, for it is unrecorded in either of the two bibliographies of the author's work that have been prepared so far, G. Evelyn Hutchinson's *A Preliminary List of the Writings of Rebecca West: 1912–1951* (1957) and the bibliography included in the volume titled *Rebecca West: A Celebration* (1977). A story that speaks boldly to issues of loss and of women's need for laughter in the face of loss, "Elegy" appears to have languished in that void where so much of women's comic writing has gone. To recover it, therefore, is to restore at least a small part of the little-known tradition of feminist philosophical humor, as well as to gain a deeper understanding of Rebecca West's early thoughts on the subject of comedy.

That West's first bibliographer, G. Evelyn Hutchinson, would not have been aware of "Elegy's" existence is puzzling. Although the story was never reprinted, it was published in a collection organized for charitable purposes that enjoyed fairly wide distribution in England by Cassell and Company and in the United States by Doubleday, Doran & Co. *The Legion Book* (1929), as this project was titled, brought together under the editorship of Captain H. Cotton Minchin contributions from authors and artists as diverse as John

Galsworthy, Edith Sitwell, and Max Beerbohm for the purpose of raising money for the British Legion. But as is the case with most such volumes produced to serve a particular function, this one disappeared from sight when its usefulness as an aid to fundraising ended. Mention of the book occurs in James McG. Stewart's *Rudyard Kipling: A Bibliographical Catalogue* (1959), but only as the site of the first publication for Kipling's poem, "The English Way." No one appears to have taken note of or remembered West's piece, not even, it would seem, West herself; evidently, she did not alert Hutchinson to its existence when he was preparing the checklist of her work, though he would thank her in print for "telling . . . [him] where much of it could be found" (Hutchinson, vi).

Even more surprising, however, is the absence of this story from the later bibliography of West's writings prepared to accompany Viking Press's *Rebecca West: A Celebration* (1977). Considering that this collection was billed on the title-page as having been "Selected from her writings by her publishers with her help," one might again have expected either the compiler of the bibliography or the author herself to have supplied the missing title. Yet, once more, there is no mention of *The Legion Book* or of "Elegy" in the section called "ANTHOLOGIES AND PUBLISHED SYMPOSIUMS TO WHICH REBECCA WEST CONTRIBUTED."

Further complicating the history of this lost story is the fact that West used the same title, "Elegy," again for her personal reminiscence of D. H. Lawrence. That piece, which first appeared as an installment of "A Letter from Abroad" in the *Bookman,* was issued in 1930 as a separate publication, then reprinted in her 1931 collection of essays called *Ending in Earnest.* It became even more widely known through its inclusion in *Rebecca West: A Celebration,* the 1977 anthology of the author's work. Therefore, it seems likely that scholars who may have happened upon mention of the earlier short story simply assumed it to be identical with the memoir of Lawrence, dated only one year later, although the two have no connection with each other.

This confusion of titles perhaps helps to explain the long silence of West's biographers, as well as bibliographers, on the question of the story's existence. Both Victoria Glendinning, in *Rebecca West: A Life* (1987), and Carl Rollyson, in the later *Rebecca West: A Saga of the Century* (1995), use the title "Elegy" to speak of the well-known memoir of D. H. Lawrence (as does Carl Rollyson again in his 1998 study, *The Literary Legacy of Rebecca West*). But neither Glendinning nor Rollyson makes reference to the other literary work of the same name.

But why should it matter to anyone that a story was lost, and that now it has been found? What makes this prodigal so significant? Obviously, the reason that the narrator gives for its importance, that "it is about Mother" (183), will not be sufficient for the average reader. The extremity of mother-worship in which the narrator indulges throughout the story is indeed affecting, but cannot be so compelling to anyone but the narrator herself. And though it may also be true that this is a story with strong autobiographical roots, grounded in the author's well-documented adoration of her own mother, whom she described in the posthumously published *Family Memories* (1987) as "magical" (218), the fact that "it is about" Isabella Fairfield will only be of interest to the tiny band of Rebecca West's biographers.

"Elegy," however, is a story that does more than describe either a single fictional mother or an actual mother and that also goes beyond the mere creation of an archetypal "Mother" figure implied by the capitalization. It is not so much "about Mother" as about the connection between the narrator's laughter and woman's social role as giver and preserver of life, about the relation in general between the comic principle and what is defined here by West as an essentialist feminine principle. Specifically, it demonstrates the terrible frailty and impermanence of women's jokes as necessary agents of morality in a male-dominated cosmos that is hostile to a moral vision. To champion life, women must laugh, both at patriarchy and at the larger realm of fatality that reflects and sustains the patriarchy's movement toward chaos. But in the short term, the joke will be on them, for the life-force succumbs and women die, regardless of such preservative labors. Whether there will be any ultimate victory, however, for the comic vision and for the women who represent it is the question that West raises here. As a story that positions life-affirming jokes by women against the backdrop of a universe in which death and loss are apportioned unjustly and as a plea for some sign that justice eventually will prevail, "Elegy" is an important precursor of West's most ambitious fictional project, an early exploration into matters at once feminist, comic, and theological that she would take up extensively in the trilogy comprising *The Fountain Overflows, This Real Night,* and *Cousin Rosamund.*[1] Though but a brief sketch for the later works, it stands as a valuable statement on such issues as what women laugh about and why it is both difficult and essential for them to keep laughing.

As in the later trilogy, the framework through which West addresses these matters is not a philosophical diatribe, but a first-person reminiscence by a female narrator, recollecting small and overlooked incidents of family history. For West, there was nothing trivial about the domestic sphere, nor was family life separate from or opposed to public life. Throughout her career, she recognized the importance of analyzing domestic relations for their political content, as staging grounds for the use and misuse of power. This was a concept she would articulate explicitly in her defense of Jane Austen from *The Court and the Castle,* a critical study of 1958, saying,

> Jane Austen has often been reproached as a chronicler of small beer on the ground that her works contain no mention of the Napoleonic wars, but . . . [she] was not apolitical, for she had much to say about those parts of the social structure which she had opportunities to observe, and notes its worst feature, which was the inequality presumed among people who were in fact equal, and who had to be dishonest to ignore their inequality. The rich despised the poor, and men despised women, and the poor were too anxious to please the rich, and women too anxious to please men. (93)

But as well as believing in narratives of family life, particularly in narratives of the hostilities between the men and women of a family, as stories with innate political meaning, West also saw them as stories with mythic significance. She herself took seriously the narrator's proposition in *Cousin Rosamund* (posthumously published, 1985) that "the world was a battlefield of forces not confined to this world" (101). In those inevitable and irreconcilable conflicts between female and male on which all her tales of family life turn, West found reflections of a cosmic struggle between the forces of good and evil. Thus, all such disputes became ennobled and mythologized in her eyes. To depict discord between the sexes in fiction was automatically to engage in an argument about competing moral values and to move into spiritual discourse. Late in life, West would assert vigorously that the duty of all art was to "have a bearing on the question which concerns us most deeply of all: whether the universe is good or bad" (*The Court and the Castle,* 5). Yet as early as 1929, West was already demonstrating in "Elegy" that a writer could examine these questions through the materials of domestic comedy—specifically, through the story of one obscure woman's attempt to outwit the men in her life, as recalled by her loving daughter.

Though the nameless woman, known only as "Mother," who is at the center of "Elegy's" plot has been dead for two years as the story opens, her influence continues to dominate the living and to shape events. In some ways, that influence is monstrous, for it has paralyzed her two grown daughters, who can see no higher purpose to their own lives than continuing the daily rituals set by her, and it has spoiled her adult son, who cannot but feel "disappointed" (183) with the more ordinary woman whom he has married. Indeed, the audience learns midway through the story that, during her own lifetime, "Mother" acknowledged with some bitterness her children's inability to move into the roles of parents themselves. But as the narrator asks, on hearing of her mother's distress over this, "[How] did she ever think we were going to marry when nobody looked at us if she was anywhere near? And how did she ever expect us to get interested in anybody when we had her!" (189). The narrator's relation to her mother certainly mirrors that of West herself, who described Isabella Fairfield as a "genius" (Rollyson, *Rebecca West*, 59) and who, according to Motley F. Deakin, "All her life . . . wanted her mother's approval for what she did, and when she did not have it she suffered and tried to obscure her failure" (Deakin, 158). Here, the fictional daughter "obscure[s] her failure" by arguing that "Maybe . . . [having Mother] kept me from other people, but maybe other people would never have made me feel sure they cared for me the way I was sure she cared for me" (190). She paints a portrait of the mother as a blameless figure too great for her environment—too loving, too generous, too creative, and too romantic—who simply could not help dwarfing her children or leaving them discontented with the less dazzling offerings of inferior human beings.

Not the least of the mother's strengths, according to the narrator's testimony, was her highly developed moral sensibility, which cut across the lines both of patriarchal law and of class boundaries. Evidence for this comes through the device that sets the narrator's recollections in motion: her receipt of a package addressed to her late mother, containing two porcelain statuettes of a shepherd and shepherdess. This present prompts a visit to the sender, a working-class woman named Annie Lumsden, who explains that her husband, shortly before his death, had wished to give something of value to the narrator's mother.[2] Although Annie Lumsden initially appears unwilling to reveal the reason for this gift, she links it to an act of kindness that the mother had performed when

> long ago there had been a dock strike which had put the whole East End out of employment, and she [Annie] and Mr. Lumsden had just been married a year then, and she was going to have a baby. After he'd been out of a job for six months he'd got quite reckless and he'd gone out . . . begging round where the houses were big. "And he went out to where your pore [sic] mother was living at the time—Muswell 'Ill, it was, and—and—" She

> couldn't go on. But I was on my feet, I was clapping my hands. For I remembered. (185–6)

The memory that Annie Lumsden reawakens in the narrator—one that has "till that minute . . . been utterly forgotten" (186)—is of herself as a small child, witnessing a kind of *tableau vivant* that she could not interpret at the time, played out between her mother and John Lumsden. Passing by the unoccupied study used by the narrator's father, Lumsden had seen the father's gold watch left lying near the open window and had entered the room to pocket it. But after catching Lumsden in the act of theft, the narrator's mother had neither turned him in to the police nor sent him on his way with a warning. Instead, she had substituted her own version of feminine justice for the conventional responses, which are linked here to masculine conduct, and had rewritten the usual plot of crime-and-punishment. Reserving her scorn for her own husband, who had tempted people to steal by flaunting his possessions, and aligning herself with the interests of the victims of a social system that gives gold watches to some and forces others to starve, the narrator's mother had not only fed the so-called criminal and taken money for him from her husband's bureau, making her a sort of transgressor herself, but had worked to ensure the survival of his family. Annie Lumsden's voice re-enters the narrative to explain,

> "She gave my husband a letter to your uncle, Mr. John Cassilis, Miss, and he made John his handyman up at his Museum of Colonial Antiques. And then he got to be janitor, and were up there till two years ago, when they let him go on a pension . . . .
>
> I wonder where I'd be now if your pore [sic] mother had sent my John to prison. I wonder where my son would be." (188–9)

Although the narrator appears never to discern the significance of John Lumsden's choice of a legacy, the reader clearly is meant to recognize the appropriateness of the gift of male and female shepherds, alluding both to the mother's pastoral role in preserving the Lumsdens and to the Christian model of the Good Shepherd whom she has emulated.

Had the story ended here, "Elegy" would have been a comic work in a broad, structural sense, as a narrative that fulfills Northrop Frye's conditions of having as its purposes "the integration of society, which usually takes the form of incorporating a central character into it" (Frye, 43) and the enactment of "deliverance from the unpleasant, even the horrible" (46). But West, as a consciously feminist author, has a very different narrative trajectory in mind, one that still leads into the realm of comedy but that neither endorses "society" nor guarantees "deliverance" from the "horrible," particularly for women. The apparent resolution to the anecdote about the rescue of the Lumsdens proves a mere blind. What the story has in fact been building toward is a further revelation and the recovery of another seemingly "forgotten" memory, showing subversive comedy as one of the best tools available to women in their struggle to shore up life, at least temporarily, against the forces of destruction and against a masculine social structure in league with those forces.

Elated by the discovery of her mother's intervention on behalf of the Lumsdens, the narrator turns to John Cassilis, her mother's brother, to praise him for what she asssumes to have been his own kindness in saving a desperate man from undeserved ruin. But Uncle John reacts with astonishment and disgust to the news that his late employee had once nearly committed a crime against property:

> "What!" He threw his pen down on the carpet and beat the air with both his fists. He has a terrible temper, it's well known in the family. "Do you mean to say this fellow was a common thief and your mother found him pilfering your father's gold watch?" (190)

As former keeper of "Colonial Antiques," Uncle John embodies a rigid and merciless legalism of the kind that had pervaded Britain's empire in the nineteenth and early twentieth centuries. His very rhetoric is that of the courtroom or the military tribunal, as he cross-examines his niece: "'Answer yes or no'" (190), he demands, a phrase about which the narrator notes with a tinge of disrespect, "He loves saying that." Even his headgear, a black skull-cap, associates him with conventional images of abstract masculine "justice," bearing a faint suggestion of the attire assumed by a judge about to condemn a prisoner to the gallows (190). Indeed, the violence of his response to the information about John Lumsden—"He was so angry that he snatched off his skull-cap and crumpled it up, and flung it in the fireplace" (191)—indicates the readiness with which he would have flung away the lives of the whole Lumsden family, as well, in the name of the law and the superior claims of property.

For a moment, both narrator and reader are left in an equal state of bafflement, unable to imagine why he had agreed to hire Lumsden in the first place. But Uncle John himself supplies the answer:

> "I'd have you know that your mother said in that letter of recommendation that she'd employed him as handyman herself for eight years and found him thoroughly respectable! She knew I wouldn't have had such a character inside the place for anything in the world! Oh, that's so like your mother!" (191)

Spurred by this information, the narrator is able at last to recover and to interpret yet another "forgotten" *tableau* from childhood, fixed upon her unconscious memory on the day when her mother had sent Lumsden to Uncle John:

> I had . . . watched my mother as she sat at her writing-table . . . first she had gazed in front of her, and tapped her pen on the inkwell, the way people do when they are pondering what to write, and then she had started, as if she had an idea, and—oh, I could hear and see it quite distinctly across the thirty-five years or so—she broke into a long, low chuckle. My naughty little mother! who had a husband like Father and a brother like Uncle John, and . . . [had] made Uncle John give a home to such a man, for all his principles, and chuckled as she did it! (191)

The implications of such an epiphanic moment are fascinating, both for the subject of women and writing in general and for the issue of women's comic writing in particular. What the narrator-as-witness reports is a scene of creative activity that involves a middle-class woman writer using her imagination in the service of aiding and preserving others, especially those who stand outside the circle of economic and social power. The lie that she invents—or, in other words, the fictional text that she produces—upholds a morality that transcends those oppressive categories of judgment (e.g., "a common thief") established by the men who control the working classes, as well as the women of their own class (and, who, as keepers of "Colonial Antiques," have also exploited the women and men of other nations and races). West's vision in "Elegy" of a woman writing fiction is of someone who is and must be, to use the phrase that Adrienne Rich made famous through the title of an essay, "Disloyal to Civilization." The mother plays deliberately upon masculine expectations about writing—the belief, for instance, that a letter of recommendation is an objective, factual document, rather than a fictional text which one must decode carefully—as well as masculine assumptions about women, who are expected to side with the interests of their own ruling social class.

But the particular genre in which the writer-figure here accomplishes her aims and the spirit in which she does so is a comic one. As she snatches the

Lumsdens from the social mechanism of ruin and "chuckles" over the means of salvation, she is both a mother and a mother-wit. With only pen, inkwell, and ingenuity as weapons, she herself sets in motion a comic plot that results in the survival of the Lumsdens and in the eventual frustration of Uncle John, the "senex" of the story, who can do nothing more than erupt in impotent fury. "Elegy" glorifies the image of the female comedian as at once saint and trickster and revels in the double-faced nature of women's laughter, as "naughty" and divine. That Rebecca West managed to insert this joke aimed at overturning the institututions of masculine authority into *The Legion Book,* a volume published to benefit the military and dedicated to the Prince of Wales as royal patron of the British Legion, is itself a wonderful feminist jest. The collection is, in a sense, subtly undermined from within by the presence of her story in it. Certainly, "Elegy" works most clearly against the spirit of contributions such as the reverent tribute by Winston Churchill to Earl Haig, as one whose "life had been given to the study of his profession" as a soldier of the Empire—a paen that erases all mention of Lord Haig's wife and children and that subsumes them into the unimportant category of the "private life" into which he "disappeared," following his military career (Churchill, 21). West's "Elegy" counters such trivializing of the "private" realm associated with the feminine by exposing the moral bankruptcy of the public realm of masculinity, militarism, and imperialism. At the same time, however, the story serves as a reminder of the existence of the women and children who make up the families of the men of the Legion; they, too, as the storystrongly suggests, must be honored and helped materially. And, of couse, they must also benefit from the funds raised by the sale of *The Legion Book.* Thus, the joke here is not one that merely aims to ridicule masculine values; on the contrary, it also encourages the formation of a spiritual community between the reading audience and all those who may be subordinate and dependent—a community that can then result in material aid.

The laughter of the mother—and, hence, of any woman who outwits the masculine social system—radiates outward and downward through time in a kind of unstoppable ripple. As the narrator announces, after her encounter with Uncle John, "I can't stop laughing. Partly because I can still hear Mother's chuckle, and when she laughed every one else wanted to laugh too" (191). What is more, the mother's own much-admired disloyalty to civilization echoes still in the spirit of the daughter, who introduces herself as one "behaving so badly" (183). The process of breaking free of the confines of masculine law continues.

Yet the comic victory at the end of West's narrative is by no means a complete one. It is not, for one thing, a victory that the mother herself enjoys first-hand. Though the mirth they generate may later prove contagious, women who use comedy as their vehicle to upset the social order must work, according to West, in secret and alone. As "Elegy" demonstrates, there is often no one with whom they can share their jokes. They move through domestic life as outsiders, alienated from those who take seriously the laws of property and of propriety. Like the late Mrs. Wilcox of E. M. Forster's *Howards End* (1910), who is censured by her husband and children for leaving a note willing her house to a friend, female moralists risk being rejected even by loved ones as "treacherous and absurd," if they are found out (Forster, 99). Appreciating at last the full extent of her mother's philosophical and emotional distance from the members of her own family, the narrator of "Elegy" cries in sympathetic anguish, "Oh, my poor mother, how she was surrounded by strangers all her days!" (191).

But the victory of the comic spirit is also incomplete, because it is only temporary; the mother has not been able to save either John Lumsden or herself from death, or her own beloved daughter from grief and loss. The very title of the story announces that its subject matter is as much lamentation as laughter. In "Elegy," Rebecca West weighs the possibility of making small gains through comedy to counter an unjust social order against the impossibility of outwitting a seemingly disordered cosmos. She uses her first-person narrator's observations to introduce this cosmic context early in the narrative, during the visit to Annie Lumsden, who is mourning the loss of her husband: "[Annie's] poor old eyes were swollen with weeping. That's one of the things that make me feel there isn't any sense in anything, the way people that other people are fond of are allowed to die" (185). Later in the story, the reader discerns from the narrator's mention of "her withered old face on the pillow" (188) that the mother's death was probably not an easeful one. The universe seems to dole out illness, suffering, and death with no more consideration of merit than the patriarchal social system uses to apportion jobs and gold watches. Certainly, the narrator herself reaches this conclusion in the closing sentences of "Elegy," as she reveals to the audience the dual explanation behind her uncontrollable laughter, with which the story begins and ends:

> I can't stop laughing. Partly because I can still hear Mother's chuckle, and when she laughed every one else wanted to laugh too. And partly because it seems so funny that people like Uncle John go on and on living, and it's two years since Mother died. (191)

Here the word "funny" takes on a tragic resonance, and the laughter of women registers as an angry protest against fate. By the end, the story's opening sentence, in which the narrator speaks of herself as "shrieking with laughter," acquires a sinister double meaning. Women, as "Elegy" suggests, will and should go on making jokes at the expense of patriarchy, but they must also recognize the limits of their own power as comic authors. Ultimately, the universe that West constructs in this story is a nihilistic place, hostile to the forces of morality embodied by women and friendly to the arbitrariness and cruelty that patriarchy embraces. No divine laughter echoes from above in response to women's humor. In this early example of West's theological thinking, there is no sign of a watchful Good Shepherd or Shepherdess beyond the "two little china figures . . . about a hundred years [old] . . . very ordinary in design" (184) preserved by John Lumsden—figures as anachronistic and impotent as the gimcrack Venus and Apollo that Sue Bridehead treasures in Hardy's *Jude the Obscure*. The only course of action the story can recommend is helpless laughter, with full knowledge that such laughter is also "helpless" in any larger sense. And the sole consolation that a woman who employs the comic perspective can take is in hoping at least that the audience which eventually hears her jokes will share her laughter, so that "every one else . . . [will] laugh too" (191).

But who is the audience for this feminist tragicomedy? "Elegy" begins with the narrator's direct address to "you" and ends with a question ("this is ever so far from Eaton Place, isn't it?" 191) posed rhetorically to a nameless and disembodied auditor, drawing the reader into the narrative but giving no clue as to what that imagined reader would be like. Eleven years earlier in her first published novel, *The Return of the Soldier* (1918), West had fantasized about the potential of an all-knowing mother figure to create a "magic circle" that would embrace the spiritually frail and dispossessed characters within the text and that might, by implication, widen to include the reader outside of the text.[3] West's interest in using texts to generate a community of sentiment shows her own grounding in the literary ideals of the Victorian period (she was born in 1892), a period she would later celebrate in the historical memoir called *1900*, published in 1982. Her eagerness to bridge the distance between the story and its reader, and between the emotions experienced by the fictional characters and those experienced by the audience, places her firmly in the tradition of Victorian storytelling, despite experiments in the decade of the Twenties with modernist form, especially in the collection of prose pieces called *The Strange Necessity* (1928). But to what sorts of assumptions and principles does the reader of "Elegy" have to assent in order to enter West's comic community and to become part of the "magic circle" of laughter that is populated by the mother, the narrator, and the author herself?

Throughout her long life, the foundation of West's thinking remained her belief in the separateness of women from men, of the female principle from the male, a separateness enacted in every human sphere, from the physical to the political to the spiritual. For West, the division between female and male mirrored an ineluctable binary opposition in creation itself—what Peter Wolfe, in *Rebecca West: Artist and Thinker* (1971), has labeled her "familiar dualist equation" (109). In all matters, gender equalled destiny, reflecting a difference between the sexes that was both constituted naturally and constructed socially in equal measure. Though formulated decades earlier in the milieu of *The Freewoman* and other pro-suffrage journals for which she wrote in the 'teens of this century, West's feminist creed comes very close to the position articulated in the 1980s by so-called "standpoint" feminists in the United States, such as Carol Gilligan and Nancy Chodorow. A similar idea can be found in Bettina Aptheker's *Tapestries of Life* (1989), a polemic which begins with the principle that

> women have a distinct way of seeing and interpreting the world. This is not to say that all women have the same consciousness or share the same beliefs. It is to say that women of each particular culture or group have a consciousness, a way of seeing, which is common to themselves as women in that it is distinct from the way the men of their culture or group see things. (12)

In work after work of fiction and non-fictional journalism, West wrote about the difference of the woman's consciousness from the man's in a manner that was certainly accessible to male readers, but by no means welcoming to them. She would, on the contrary, have been proud to be named a precursor to those late-twentieth-century feminists who proposed the existence of a separate epistemological framework shared only by women—one that, moreover, takes "a critical stance in relation to rationality, objectivity, and universality, asserting the significance and legitimacy of emotional, politically engaged, and particularistic ways of knowing" (Kemp and Squires, 142). But such a posture also helps explain why, as Bonnie Kime Scott notes, "West has been found unsatisfactory" by other schools of "recent feminists," who are offended by her "consistent recourse to conflictual binaries, [and] her focus upon heterosexual relations," as well as her "ambivalence regarding homosexuality" (Scott, *Refiguring Modernism*, 125). These feminists have "queered" the very divisions that West preferred to think of in absolute terms. In her view, the gendering of human beings into male and female was not a social operation, but a "natural" and irresistible one, permeating and determining every response.

For West, moreover, the distinction between the female and male "way of seeing" and between women and men was not one of neutral value. She insisted, as Motley F. Deakin puts it, that "women are superior to men" (109). There was, as she wrote in a letter from 1968 quoted by Victoria Glendinning's biography of West, "something so desperately unlovable, even unlikeable, about the male sex" (235)—something perhaps related to the unmerited political advantage of gender, to what Carl Rollyson describes as the fact that "men were given privileges largely because they were men, not because they were inherently superior to women" (Rollyson, *Literary Legacy*, 223). And just as her narrative vision of how fiction could create a community of feeling between a text and its reader owed much to Victorian literary theory, so her notion of the sources of female superiority lay in Victorian social ideology. Despite her sincere, lifelong insistence upon women's need for political and economic equality, West continued to ascribe to a Ruskinian ideal of women as Angels, whose natural direction was upward. Indeed, in the very year that also saw the publication of "Elegy," West had illustrated this proposition in the fantasy-novel called *Harriet Hume* (1929), which ends with its all-wise heroine leading her flawed and murderous male lover, who is described throughout as her archetypal "opposite," heavenwards to "A Very Happy Eternity" (*Harriet Hume*, 288). To quote Harold Orel's summary of West's linkage of morality with gender:

> Women replenish the race; they have healthy and vital instincts; though undervalued, put down, ignored, they remind us of the sanity that is essential for the progress of civilisation. Men, on the other hand, pillage, torture, and kill in ways and for reasons that remain forever mysterious to the feminine mind . . . . [The] male drift [is] toward death. (77)

Thus, to laugh along with, rather than at, the central joke of "Elegy," one must be willing to subscribe to West's theory that women alone are the moral centers of the universe and that they are better than men—not superior merely to misguided individual men of the upper-class patriarchy, such as "Father" and the stiff-necked imperialist, "Uncle John," but to all men. Even John Lumsden, the working-class man who proves his virtue by being ready to "steal for his woman when she was hungry" (191), appears not to be fully exempt from this blanket condemnation. By giving Lumsden the same first name as both Uncle John and the narrator's married brother, West manages to suggest that all men, regardless of class and character, may be interchangeable in the end. Moreover, the very facility with which John Lumsden steps into the patriarchal and imperialistic system when given the opportunity, keeping up the Museum of Colonial Antiques and finishing life as someone "looked up to" (189), casts doubt upon his initial status as a symbol of moral rebellion against the social order. The working-class man, too, it would seem, is ready both to prop up and to share in the power of the middle- and upper-class masculine hierarchy. Only the narrator's mother somehow retains the special purity of the outsider, with the right to laugh at that order (although, to accept the mother as a social rebel, one must disregard the fact that she employs a staff of servants and thus enjoys unreflectively the privileges of her own class position). And West appears to invite only the reader who shares this same feminine perspective to laugh along with her—reaching out, in particular, to a female reader who, as a daughter herself, identifies with the narrator's wish to recover and to celebrate mother-wit.

The issue of laughter, therefore, in this story comes along with a series of problems, ranging from limitations upon the power of the female comedian within the setting of the cosmos to limitations in the size of the potential community that her laughter can generate on this earth. What West does not question here, however, is the existence or the survival of the ability to laugh; indeed, the narrative shows the comic perspective being passed on from mother to daughter in a process of renewal. In 1929, West still believed in renewal. The experience of the First World War had shaken but not smashed her faith that the world would go on. Although she uses the story titled "Elegy" to rail against the injustice of mortality, against the fact that meritorious individuals must die, there is no sign here of the bleak political conclusion at which she would arrive following the Second World War—that life itself soon might end altogether, wiped out by a nuclear holocaust brought on by male leaders in love with the power of destruction.

It was, perhaps, because of just such an evolution in her thinking that West was willing to allow this short story to remain lost and forgotten, or at least to do nothing during her own lifetime to enter it into the official canon of her bibliography. Just as she would later turn her attention from questions of individual mortality to matters concerning the doubtful future of the human race, so she would become increasingly dissatisfied with fiction, including her own fiction, that seemed too focused upon the personal. In the ten years following the publication of "Elegy," the sequence of international events leading up to the World War II would convince her of the dangers of concentrating excessively either upon one's own private sphere—a condition which, in her two-volume opus of 1942, *Black Lamb and Grey Falcon*, she would label "idiocy"—or upon the sphere of public affairs alone—the condition she would mock as "lunacy" (*Black Lamb and Grey Falcon*, 3). In order to perform their functions as artists and as social beings responsibly, writers (and women writers, in particular) would have to bring together the concerns of the private and the public, as West herself first attempted in *Black Lamb and Grey Falcon* and continued to do in her post-World War II narrative sequence of *The Fountain Overflows*, *This Real Night*, and *Cousin Rosamund*. In that ambitious final series of novels, to which the author herself referred as "A Saga of the Century," West could set against the full backdrop of twentieth-century British history those issues which she had merely been able to sketch out in "Elegy"—issues such as how women's laughter intersects with the subjects of divine justice and human destiny.

Along with her increasing shift toward a merger of the personal with the public in her choice of literary subject matter, another influence upon West's decision to leave "Elegy" in obscurity might have been her changing attitude toward laughter itself. Throughout her life, West proved adept at working in comic modes, whenever she chose to do so. Gifted at making others laugh, she was, in the view of Bonnie Kime Scott, by nature a "witty raconteur" who could produce, for the benefit of friends, letters that were "extremely funny" and that had those who read them "rolling on the floor" (Scott, *Letters*, xix). Nevertheless, during the later years of her career, West came to question the most basic assumption with which comedy traditionally has begun and on which it has for centuries depended—that renewal and regeneration will go on, whether in human nature or in external nature, and that winter will be succeeded by spring. In *Anatomy of Criticism* (1957), the classic essay in archetypal criticism, Northrop Frye pointed to the vital links between the comic spirit and belief in a "green world" produced by the "victory of summer over winter" (183). For Frye, all literature is tied to cyclical movement, but in comedy in particular "time plays a redeeming role: it uncovers and brings to light what is essential to the happy ending" (213).

As Rebecca West, however, began in the 1950s to look back upon the course of twentieth-century political history, it seemed to her that such confidence in time as a positive agent was no longer possible. In the last book published before her death, the autobiographical meditation upon life at the turn of the century titled *1900*, West would date the beginnings of a widely felt uncertainty about the survival both of British civilization and of the planet itself to the end of Queen Victoria's reign. A figure symbolic of abundant fertility and motherhood, Queen Victoria had functioned, according to West, as a nature goddess outside the political realm, a signifier of perpetuity:

> I can vouch for it that . . . a queen is in some mystical way more real than a king. We know that she has all these children. We know that the seasons of the year repeat themselves and that, usually, fruitfulness has the last word. That was the reassurance Queen Victoria gave nineteenth-century Britain . . . . [When she died] We also grieved because the element of continuity, the promise that life would never stop, did not seem quite such a firm guarantee. (*1900*, 180–81)

No longer did West view the loss of a mother-figure as merely a personal grief with merely personal consequences, as she had treated the subject in "Elegy," but as a mythic portent of the disruption of natural cycles. Yet to announce her doubt "that the seasons of the year repeat themselves" and to foresee the cessation of these cycles of renewal was also to jeopardize any possibility of writing fiction that employed a comic structure or that validated women's laughter.

This is a problem that West did not address in "Elegy," her early meditation upon the feminist comic spirit, but one which she took up as a central issue in her later trilogy of *The Fountain Overflows* (1956), *This Real Night* (posthumously published, 1984), and *Cousin Rosamund* (posthumously published, 1985). Looking back upon "Elegy" from the vantage point of her mature reconsideration of history, West might well have felt that she had framed her argument in 1929 about women's comic responses naively or at least incompletely. Certainly, in the opening volume of that trilogy (the only one of the series actually published during her lifetime), West would dramatize the dilemma faced by a female consciousness that has become aware of the helplessness of maternal figures to ensure the continuance of the natural cycles and that has, as a result, lost the ability to laugh or to delight in seeing others do so.

In a key scene from *The Fountain Overflows* for the question of women's comedy, the narrator, a child named Rose Aubrey living at the turn of the century, records the philosophical struggle between her mother and father as they clash over the subject of the earth's future:

> In the night, in our bedroom, we had wondered whether there was anything to prevent the world from deciding that it would not wake up and have a spring, and then everybody would get colder and colder, and the days would go on getting shorter and shorter, and in the end there would be only darkness. We asked Papa and Mamma about this, and Papa said, "Well, it might happen, but not in your time."
>
> "But we don't want it to happen at all," said Cordelia.
>
> "Do not frighten the children," said Mamma. "Spring has always come, so we can take it that it will always come."
>
> "What an argument for a fellow-countrywoman of David Hume," said Papa. Nobody has ever upset his contention that though certain causes produce a certain effect on one occasion, this gives no logical proof that they are bound to produce it on another. "We may yet see universal and eternal night." He gave one of his grating laughs. "But I do not think you children need worry about it." Yet we worried because we obscurely felt that he felt a certain delight in contemplating a never-ending winter, chill and darkness never to be dispelled. It did not matter that Mamma told us then, and often later, that day and spring were bound to come, for we sometimes suspected that he had the greater power. (*The Fountain Overflows*, 128–9)

Pondering the fact not merely that she as an individual is mortal, but that "the world might stop totally" (178), Rose becomes overwhelmed by a sense of paralyzing anxiety. In the face of the masculine prediction of a future of "nothingness and nothingness and nothingness" (178)—a forecast that is as much a threat as a prediction, since men have the "greater power" politically to make this promise come true—the narrator loses her own faith in the formula which has allowed her to go on this far, her talismanic chant that "in the end we would be all right" (178). As Rose explains in despair, "But we would have to have a framework in which to be all right, and about that I was no longer certain" (178).

Without a philosophical "framework in which to be all right," there is no guarantee of a narrative framework in which, as Frye puts it, "time plays a redeeming role." Hence, comedy itself becomes problematic. As was not true in the more simplistic "Elegy," laughter in *The Fountain Overflows* assumes a multi-sided, thorny, and even menacing character. Indeed, the figures most often associated with laughter in the later novel are male—men who use the exercise of wit as a device to spread ruin, to express their delight in the destruction they have wreaked, and to distance themselves from the consequences (both material and psychological) that their actions have produced upon the women around them. Such a wielder of comedy as a form of weaponry is Jock, a cousin of Rose's mother, who carries out his "determination to be funny though . . . [he] could not think of anything really funny to say" (115) by mocking and humiliating his wife and daughter. When he is challenged by Rose's mother, who confronts him, asking, "'Jock, why must you play the clown? . . . Why must you try to spoil everything?'" (338), his answer is a kind of self-deluded, masculine existentialist's defense: "'Life is so terrible. There is nothing to do with it but break it down into nonsense'"(338), he replies, never recognizing or admitting that his own actions make life more "terrible," especially for the women who must be dependent upon him.

Even the far more appealing and glamorous character of "Papa," the narrator's father, is guilty of turning comedy into "sneering laughter" (141) and of using the comic principle in the service of destruction, rather than affirmation. His is a "wit . . . which turned things upside down" (72), and in the absence of any assurance that there is a higher power waiting to right them again, such an act of masculine aggression through comedy becomes immensely sinister. Indeed, the word "grating," the adjective which the narrator connects to his laughter, suggests that comedy here is something that no longer deflects pain, as it did in "Elegy," but instead that produces it, by rubbing against and wearing away the lives of women in particular.

In the context of the more complex and elaborate treatment of comedy at which Rebecca West arrived some twenty-five-years later in *The Fountain Overflows*, even the laughter of women, which in "Elegy" had seemed a wholly positive response to circumstances, assumes a mixed and troubling character. Rose Aubrey, the philosophically tormented narrator of the novel, rarely laughs; however, her less intellectual and more intuitively wise cousin, Rosamund, does retain her comic perspective. Rosamund's defense against the sneering assaults of her father, Jock, is to dismiss him with a "lazy smile" (332). It is the only questionable stance ever taken by this otherwise seemingly flawless, almost angelic, protagonist. As the narrator comments, in some perplexity over the morality of Rosamund's attitude, "I was prepared to think it right that Rosamund should hate her father, but not that she should regard him with what seemed to me a hard and frivolous amusement" (332). Rose ultimately will decide that mockery, even in the hands of so virtuous a character as Rosamund, is an unacceptable tactic: "You did not hit people below the belt or take from them their seriousness" (342).

Elsewhere, too, laughter, though especially at the expense of others, seems to present itself as a temptation that women must try to resist. When, for instance, the narrator's untalented sister, Cordelia, is pushed by an adoring teacher into a career as a violinist and into a demonstration of her musical skills for her family, the ability to suppress the comic impulse becomes a moral test for "Mamma," Rose and Cordelia's mother:

> Then suddenly we were afraid, for she began to laugh. We watched in terror while she and her laughter contended like two desperate people wrestling on the edge of an abyss, for Cordelia and Miss Beevor [her teacher] really did not deserve that, nobody deserved that. She won just in time to be able to turn slowly as the last note sounded and say in an unhurried voice, "Cordelia, what a lovely Christmas present" . . . . (98)

By the time she had begun her novelistic trilogy in the mid-1950s—exactly the same time, as it happened, that G. Evelyn Hutchinson was assembling the first bibliography of her published works—Rebecca West's thoughts on the issue of comedy had evolved in many ways from their early incarnation in "Elegy." No longer could she endorse comedy so positively as a strategy for women, for she had lost the very confidence in futurity, in the assumption that this world would still be here from one moment to the next, on which the comic spirit rests. (And it was, perhaps, for this reason that she found it impossible ever to finish the full sequence of her "Saga of the Century," abandoning the project before the end of her life and leaving it to her literary executors to piece together the material that has been published as *This Real Night* and *Cousin Rosamund*.) In her creative maturity, she had, moreover, come to acknowledge that as well as being an agent for sanity and morality, laughter carried a far greater potential to be hurtful and "sneering," even when employed by women. Thus, in thinking back upon "Elegy," as she must have done in both 1957 and 1977 when approached by bibliographers seeking her help in identifying all her published works, Rebecca West might well have decided to engage in an act of self-censorship, feeling that the story had little of value to offer a later-twentieth-century audience.

Whatever her reasons might have been, however, for impeding or at least delaying the study of "Elegy" by readers and scholars, West's judgment about it has proved wrong. Though modest in its reach, the 1929 story remains an affecting *cri de coeur* and also an important *rire de coeur*. And despite the author's own silence as to the existence of "Elegy," which she seems to have maintained for over five decades, it is good to be able at last to add its ghostly feminist "chuckle" to the roar of twentieth-century British women's laughter. Those of us who do choose to continue to believe in futurity have gained one more voice to help encourage us on our way.

NOTES

1. Although what exists now is a trilogy, Victoria Glendinning suggests in the "Afterword" to West's posthumously published *Cousin Rosamund* that the author may originally have had a four-novel sequence in mind for her uncompleted saga about the twentieth century as experienced by the Aubrey family. For more about West's intentions, see *Cousin Rosamund*, 287–95.

2. It is interesting to note that West had already made similar use of this device of the visit of a middle-class narrator to a working-class household to gain information about a loved one as the stimulus to the plot in her earlier novel, *The Return of the Soldier* (1918).

3. For more about Rebecca West's obsessive concern with the "magic circles" created by maternal love, see Margaret D. Stetz, "Drinking 'The Wine of Truth': Philosophical Change in West's *Return of the Soldier*," in *Arizona Quarterly* 43.1 (1987): 63–78.

CHAPTER THREE

The Ghost and Mrs. Muir: Laughing with the Captain in the House

For the women of Britain, 1945 must have been a year filled with ghosts: ghosts of dead soldier sons, brothers, fathers, husbands, and lovers; ghosts of the lives they had led before the war, smashed into atoms along with the 475,000 houses totally destroyed by bombs dropped during the Blitz (Stevenson, 448); ghosts of their own former selves—selves that had believed in the possibility of peace and security. Many of these women must have felt haunted, as Vera Brittain had at the end of the previous World War, when she had wandered the environs of Oxford alone, obsessed with remembrances of her brother and fiance, both killed in action:

> The two of them seemed to fuse in my mind into a kind of composite lost companion, an elusive ghost which embodied all intimacy, all comradeship, all joy, which included everything that was the past and should have been the future. Incessantly I tramped across the Hill, subconsciously pursuing this symbolic figure like a lost spirit seeking for its mate . . . . (Brittain, 485)

In the disorienting aftermath of that earlier war, Vera Brittain had experienced a breakdown of the psychic barriers between the actual and the supernatural, seeing before her not only the forms of desired figures who were not there, but impossible transformations of her own body:

> I looked one evening into my bedroom glass and thought, with a sense of incommunicable horror, that I detected in my face signs of some sinister and peculiar change. A dark shadow seemed to lie across my chin; was I beginning to grow a beard, like a witch? (484)

Surely many of the women who emerged from the nightmare of the Second World War, especially those who had also lived through the First, felt themselves similarly caught in a liminal world, a place inhabited by spectres.

For such women, gothic conventions and metaphors provided the nearest equivalent to a language with which to describe that mental state and to render its strangeness more familiar. But it was gothic comedy or mock-gothic narrative that could offer the safest framework through which to acknowledge this condition of being "haunted" and yet to allay the terrors attached to that recognition. Although Sybil Korff Vincent may claim in "The Mirror and the Cameo: Margaret Atwood's Comic/Gothic Novel, *Lady Oracle*" that Atwood "created a new sub-genre—the comic/Gothic" as late as 1976 to express the anxieties of female readers (Vincent, 153), Atwood's work actually follows in an existing tradition that had embraced and revised the gothic form to help an earlier generation of women to regain their sense of control.

Thus it was to the popular comic-gothic novel *The Ghost and Mrs. Muir* that large numbers of British and American readers turned for solace and relief in 1945. In that novel, Josephine Leslie, an Englishwoman writing under the ambiguously gendered pseudonym of "R. A. Dick," encouraged her female audience to accept as both real and as beneficent the ghosts that populated their minds and to draw comfort from these presences. When Joseph Mankiewicz directed his Hollywood film version of *The Ghost and Mrs. Muir* in 1947, with a screenplay by Philip Dunne, he emphasized the role of the phantasm as a romantic substitute or consolation, a role that the author herself had to some degree endorsed. As Frieda Grafe phrases this, in a monograph for the British Film Institute, "The ghost was not to turn up as a frightening spook, but as a male dream-being" (Grafe, 17). But Leslie's original work also had a more subversive intent: to urge her audience to use their ghosts as inspirations for creativity and as allies in a rebellion against ideological forces that were acting to regulate and circumscribe women's lives. What readers found in this novel was not so much a romantic ghost as a laughing one. With the help of this defiant, satirical figure, they could learn to ridicule the new feminine ideal toward which they were being aggressively pushed at the War's end. This was a ghost who allowed women to uncover, among other things, their sexual androgyny and "masculine" potential for independence, adventure, and self-definition, and who taught them to prefer the company of their own unfettered imaginations to the coercive situations of social life. At a time when feminism itself seemed all but dead and feminist art along with it, Josephine Leslie kept the ghost of an earlier movement alive in the realm of popular fiction—where, indeed, it could do the most good, through the broadest possible circulation.

That there was a market for comedy of the supernatural in wartime England had been demonstrated by the success of Noel Coward's *Blithe Spirit,* which opened in London in 1941 and still was being performed four years later. And though Josephine Leslie's gothic jest proved quite different in tone and content from that "blithe" fantasy, it shared with Coward's play both a grounding in a comedy-of-manners tradition that looked back to Oscar Wilde and a rigorous skepticism about the automatic equation of heterosexual marriage with domestic bliss. In *The Ghost and Mrs. Muir,* set at the turn of the century, the middle-class heroine's life begins only when her husband's ends. After she moves herself and her two children to a house by the sea, the ghost that she encounters there is not that of her late spouse (as it was in Coward's plot), but the spirit of an unfamiliar male alter-ego, a seafarer who has led the life of adventure denied to those of her sex and class. With the encouragement of this presence that may also be a projection of her own suppressed "masculine" ambitions and need for self-assertion, she writes a bestseller, handles her own business arrangements, supports her children, and extricates herself from all social and erotic relationships that make her unhappy. At the end of the novel which follows her through to old age and death, the two halves of herself—the "lady" and the "Captain"—that would have been prohibited from uniting in the social world embrace at last in an afterworld.

Coming out in the latter half of the 1940s, Leslie's novel posed a brave challenge in a climate of growing unfriendliness toward women who might seek contentment through work, solitude, or the pursuit of pleasures that did not lead to a rise in the population. In Britain, as in the United States, the end of the War was accompanied by a concerted effort on the part of political and cultural authorities to turn workers into homemakers, unmarried women and widows into wives, wives into mothers, and mothers into full-time caretakers of others. As Jane Lewis has said, in defining what she terms the "familialist ideology" of the period, England was rapidly becoming a

> postwar society in which concern about the level of the birth rate had not yet been overtaken by evidence of a baby boom (just as married women's work had not yet been legitimized by evidence of the increasing numbers of wives engaged in it); in which doctors, social workers, social scientists, magistrates and politicians all expressed their desire to see the family 're-built" on traditional lines; and in which academics led the way in condemning the effect of married women's work on children's development. (Lewis, 178)

So seriously did the British government take its role in ensuring that women accept their destinies as breeders and nurturers that a Royal Commission on Population was appointed in 1944 to determine what they "required [as] encouragement from the state to remain at home and rear children" (Pugh, 158). The result of the Commission's investigations was approval of family allowances and other "welfare measures enacted after 1945 . . . designed to support woman in her capacity as wife and mother" (Pugh, 158). The new postwar "welfare state," Sheila Rowbotham notes in her comprehensive history *A Century of Women,* was not really "new" at all in its gender ideology, for it "was based on the assumption of women's dependence on the man in the family rather than on women's rights as individuals" (Rowbotham, 247). Thus, as Martin Pugh has summarized the situation, in an atmosphere where governmental bodies and social institutions agreed upon the urgency for a return to the largely discarded model of the docile, fecund Angel in the House, "the popular purveyors of the domestic cult flourished as never before, the political parties intensified their existing strategies for women, and organized feminism continued its apparently inexorable decline" (159).

With the War drawing to its conclusion, women who had been told to keep the homefires burning were now being ordered to turn them into pyres. On these they were to immolate both the ghosts of lost loved ones and the ghosts of their own desires for anything that did not promote the domestic ideal, the better to get on with the business of marriage, remarriage, and procreation. In 1946, the most popular British "woman's picture" was David Lean's *Brief Encounter,* a film that applauded its heroine for putting aside her romantic yearnings toward a man other than her husband, for overcoming her impulse to commit suicide in the face of permanent separation from her lover, and for returning from the adventurous transience of the railway cafe to the staid, upholstered sitting-room that represented married life. To do otherwise, as the screenplay adapted from a short story by Noel Coward implied, would be to behave selfishly. Such selfishness in a woman was, according to the prevailing ideology of the day, more than merely unfeminine; it was a betrayal of one's class—of the stiff-upper-lip restraint that had defined middle-class virtue throughout the perils of the Blitz—and also a betrayal of one's country. As in the nineteenth century, when wife and home were held by Victorian culture to be the reward earned by weary Empire-builders, so at the end of the Second World War, women were encouraged to subordinate their own wishes to those of the tired soldiers, who had been dreaming of domestic idylls past and future. Being a "good" wife and mother became a patriotic duty, a way of showing gratitude to the newly demobbed. As Niamh Baker writes in *Happily Ever After? Women's Fiction in Postwar Britain,1945–60,*

> The pleasures of home life, of living once again in a family, particularly as the head of that family, must have come as a welcome relief to men returning from war. A woman safely at home, keeping that home ready for the man's return from daily work, is an appealing arrangement. It also gave men a greater sense of security: the upsets of war could be forgotten, and life would go on, as far as family relationships were concerned, as it always had done. (Baker, 19)

But were the desires of all women, in these matters, the same as those of some postwar heterosexual men? Did each and every one of them long merely for quietude, forgetfulness, and immersion in family life? The popularity of Josephine Leslie's novel would suggest otherwise, for *The Ghost and Mrs. Muir* gives hope, through its gothic comedy, to those who would preserve their restless, disturbing memories and their impulses toward autonomy. With an obstreporous ghost by her side, to support her in her resistance, Leslie's middle-class heroine evades all attempts by well-meaning and not so well-meaning women and men alike to control her. She uses her widowhood—the condition of which an acquaintance speaks grimly as "living alone without a man's protection" (Leslie, *Ghost,* 11)—as an opportunity to discover her own multiple identities, which include those of author, mother, house-restorer, passionate lover, philanthropist, and even speculator about the afterworld. All of these selves become available to her once she has taken the first step of accepting the masculine persona who inhabits her consciousness in the form of a ghost, laughing and chuckling to her in a voice that "she did not hear . . . with her ears . . . [but that] seemed to come straight into her mind like thought" (30). And just as the heroine slips the social bonds, so the novel itself escapes the confines of the marriage plot typical of popular writings for women. In search of an alternative, it invokes the ghost of an earlier kind of fiction—the "New Woman" novel of the turn of the century, as produced by both female and male authors—and allows that narrative, rather than the exigencies of conventional romance, to shape the course of events.

Exposing the inadequacies of the romance plot is a project that Josephine Leslie takes up explicitly and immediately in *The Ghost and Mrs. Muir*—indeed, within the opening paragraphs. The narrative begins with the recognition by Lucy Muir, the newly widowed, thirtyish heroine, that the years of her marriage were ones in which "her life had [not] been unhappy, it had just not been her life at all . . . . Even at night her life had been entirely Edwin's, and not her own, in the large double bed where his unfortunate habit of snoring shook even her dreams into his pattern" (4–5). She had entered into this marriage at the age of seventeen, spurred less by love than by her naive faith in the correspondence between reality and literature and in the prophetic power of romantic fiction:

> [She] had been reading a novel at the time in which the hero had had a fair lock of hair falling over his forehead. Edwin's hair had grown in the same way . . . . The novel finished with a kiss in the rose garden, and the magic words, 'and so they lived happily ever after,' and Lucy Muir, having been kissed in the orchard, could see no other ending to her own romance. (4)

But age and experience correct this early inability to separate facts from romantic illusions and also teach her the necessity of devising new kinds of stories for herself, in order to determine her own fate. Midway through the narrative, Lucy Muir becomes entangled, at the age of thirty-four, with Miles Blane, who captures her by posing as the stereotypical hero of a romance, world-weary and ready to be redeemed by her goodness. What he does not reveal about himself is that he already has a wife and children and, moreover, that he has a mistress who visits him in the seaside cottage where he supposedly lives alone. When Lucy discovers him with this mistress, she experiences the revelation as though it were occurring in a third-rate melodrama, at which she is a mere spectator:

> [The] lamp-lit scene held as little reality for her as if it were, indeed, part of a play upon a lime-lit stage . . . . And Lucy seemed to know the play by heart. She knew the woman would lean back and stare boldly . . . and though Lucy could not see his [Miles's] face, she knew that there was a stage direction there for a wink and frown of warning. (96)

Fortunately, though, by recognizing the nature of the stale and unfulfilling domestic scenario into which Miles has attempted to thrust her, she is able to graduate beyond the role of passive audience for worn, predictable fictions and, in the process, to cease to be victimized by them. She responds to Miles's acting of the part of wounded innocence by deciding to take charge, announcing that she will have no more to do with him:

> He could go from one play to another, always the central figure, always bringing down the curtain when comedy threatened to turn to tragedy or

> domesticity, leaving the other players stranded, to think out their own endings to their ruined plot; but thought Lucy, it was she who held the book of this play and she would end it in her own manner. (97)

At this moment, she assumes the mantle of authorship herself, possessed of the means to rewrite both literature and life; soon, she will also demonstrate her fitness for authorship as a profession, by producing and selling an unconventional text .

Parallelling Lucy's gradual discovery of her power to fashion her own plots and endings is her increasing decisiveness about the question of where and how she will live, about the shaping of a house for herself. The confidence to create new narrative structures seems to grow directly out of the ability to order one's own physical space, independently of the wishes of others. Rearranging the house of fiction and rearranging the domestic sphere to suit the needs of the individual woman are presented here as related acts. The late Edwin Muir had been, as we are told, an architect, responsible for the design of the pretentious "pseudo-Elizabethan house, which he had built for her as a wedding present" (3) that she is forced by debts to sell in the wake of his death. Like most everything else in their marriage, the house had been ordered not to her own specifications but to his, and had reflected, moreover, the promptings of a masculine, "public" sensibility, drawn to institutional models, rather than a feminine, "private" one, drawn to domesticity. As Lucy notes, in comparing Edwin's house to the one she chooses for herself in her widowhood, "'My husband studied architecture for years, but he never made such a satisfactory little house as this—though I believe he was very clever at prisons and post-offices'" (36). Here, scale takes on a gendered value. Unlike her late husband, Lucy can enjoy the snugness and efficiency of Gull Cottage, which she appreciates from the first as a "small, grey stone house" (10), because she herself is, as we learn in the opening sentence of the novel, "a little woman" (3). As Lucy is quick to point out, however, size is no determinant of soundness or resiliency, except under a misguided code of masculine ethics: "'I'm strong, too,' Lucy defended herself. 'It's just because I'm small that I'm considered weak'" (28). Gull Cottage, which is set on a cliff beside the sea, remains firm despite its buffettings from wind and saltwater, while Lucy herself retains her integrity and resolution in the face of every moral and social challenge.

From the beginning, Josephine Leslie asks her readers to acknowledge consciously the identification between Gull Cottage and Lucy Muir—that is, between the house and the heroine—that Lucy experiences unconsciously.

Certainly, Lucy recognizes at once the pull upon her that this house exerts, even if she cannot see its likeness to herself. When called upon by the ghostly voice of Captain Gregg, the late designer and builder of Gull Cottage, to prove that her interest in it is deeper than mere attraction to the prospect of having control of a household, she declares,

> "But I want to live in *this* house," said Lucy, "it's more *my* house than any I've ever seen" . . . . "I felt it was my place as soon as I saw it. I fell in love with it at once—I can't explain it—it was as if the house itself were welcoming me and crying out to be rescued from its degradation." (34)

Upon entering Gull Cottage, which has been abandoned since the death of its owner twelve years earlier and unsaleable due to its reputation for being haunted, Lucy notes in its furnishings a strange contradictoriness and incongruity: "It was well proportioned, but contained the oddest mixture of the beautiful and bourgeois that Lucy had ever seen" (12). In defining "bourgeois" and "beautiful" as antithetical properties, and in determining to strip from the house the former while preserving the latter, Lucy also makes, albeit unknowingly, an important decision about how she will reshape her own character, now that she is no longer Edwin Muir's wife. One product of this resolve is her eagerness to sweep away what she perceives as an atmosphere of morbidity at Gull Cottage, where "the dust and dirt lay like a shroud" (14), as though the house, too, were widowed and in enforced mourning for its late owner. Indeed, the resemblance becomes complete, at least for the reader, when Lucy speaks of the rooms as "covered with such dust and festooned with such cobwebs that the very air seemed veiled" (13), for Lucy herself is at that moment the image of "a very black-draped widow" (12), masked by "trailing black draperies, chosen for her by Helen" (5), one of the interfering sisters-in-law who has tried to make Lucy conform to social proprieties. Up until Lucy's appropriation of it, the house has succumbed to a kind of wasting illness:

> The wallpaper had gone past fading into death, turning . . . a livid mauve, against which the peeling white paint looked like something stricken with leprosy . . . [and] the grey film of dust, spreading over them [i.e., the furnishings], looked like some other foul disease. (13)

Only through this objective manifestation of the symptoms of depression, frustration, and anger does the reader become aware of the toll exacted upon

Lucy, too, from the strain of living up to the demands of others. Indeed, even at the moment when she makes her first gesture toward finding those "other ways of living that might be better suited to herself" (5) by removing herself and her children from the influence of Edwin Muir's meddlesome family and by occupying Gull Cottage, Lucy suffers from feelings of panic not unlike a devastating sickness: "Common sense and suitability and the right thing and what every one does, my dear, all clawing at her budding independence, to tear it to pieces and fling it to the four winds" (18).

Despite its general murkiness and fadedness, however, which are the signs of its psychic distemper, Gull Cottage does have one curiously bright spot:

> What took the eye in this room, and held it, was a brass telescope standing on a tripod in the window, glittering in the afternoon sun. Lucy stared at this object and stared at it again . . . . No, there was something about this particular telescope that had hit her sight with almost physical violence as soon as she had entered the room.
>
> "Of course," she said aloud, "you're clean!" (15)

What chills both Lucy and the estate agent who acts as her guide is, of course, the supernatural implication of this discovery, the possibility that someone or something has been peering through the telescope in this uninhabited house without leaving any other physical manifestation of its presence, not so much as a footprint in the undisturbed dust. But what must strike readers once again is the likeness in situation between house and heroine. Lucy, too, despite her compulsory shrouding and veiling—not merely in widow's weeds, but in the dust of those social rules and expectations that lie so chokingly upon her—has retained a kind of clean look-out, a telescope from the mind's eye aimed outward to a freer world. Through it, Lucy sees beyond the confines of her roles as "'little Mrs. Muir' or 'dear little Mrs. Muir,' and latterly as 'poor little Mrs. Muir'"(3), the names imposed upon her by others, to a future in which she will assume the persona of "Lucia," the name offered to her by the ghostly voice echoing within her consciousness. As "Lucia," she will throw off the draperies enveloping not only her body, but also her thoughts and her speech. She will refuse to be ruled any longer by the self-doubts and nervous hesitations that she has learned from those who surround her; she will recognize that to accommodate oneself over time to either the intellectual or the emotional inhibitions of others, however greatly beloved those others may be, is to descend by invisible degrees to a condition of psychic victimization and constriction more terrible than any gothic imaginings.

The resemblance between the character of the protagonist and the character of the house becomes complete when both of these structures are found to be haunted, to be the dwelling places of an unruly and disruptive force that manifests its presence through its jokes and laughter. Paranormal and comic elements merge in Lucy's very first statements of her suspicions about Gull Cottage: "'But it does suit me!' said Lucy. 'It's exactly the house I want. But there's something funny about it'" (15). Soon the sense of something "funny" in the air is confirmed by a noise at once frightening and engaging, a noise that appears to emerge simultaneously from within and without Lucy, to exist both in the house and in her private consciousness: "Another sound seemed to be filling the room and her ears, a deep rich chuckle" (16). If, at the start of the narrative, Lucy Muir is a figure already bearing the weight of sad ghosts, including the remembrance of her unsatisfying marriage and the spectre of her wasted youth, she certainly accumulates further grim charges along the way. When, for instance, she breaks off her relationship with Miles Blane, on whom has pinned her romantic hopes, Lucy experiences the terrible aspect of being haunted, as, stricken and miserable, "She sat there, staring at the ghost of her own happiness" (98). Yet the novel reminds its readers throughout that memory, imagination, and inventiveness need not be merely a curse for women, leading them to suffer their griefs and losses more acutely, but also a blessing, giving them the power to conjure up or to feel themselves possessed by buoyant and amusing spirits, who can sustain and protect them. In the consciousness of having a mocking voice as one's ally, whether or not that voice actually exists independently of oneself, lies the possibility of salvation.

This "inspiriting" potential of ghosts is nowhere more evident than in the content and structure of the novel itself, which is populated throughout by the benevolent presences of earlier British fictions, especially pro-feminist ones. Indeed, the character of Lucy Muir is a kind of layered figure, through whom the ghosts of other literary heroines are visible. Her very name suggests a composite of two questing protagonists from the works of E. M. Forster—Lucy Honeychurch, the young woman who awakens to sexual and philosophical rebellion in *A Room with a View* (1908), and Mrs. Moore of *A Passage to India* (1924), who is, near the end of her life, engaged in her own retreat from the "muddle" of bourgeois social values and in search of a passage beyond these to wisdom. Similarly, in the irreverent voice of Lucy's ghostly companion, Captain Gregg, there are echoes from the play *Heartbreak House* (1917) of Bernard Shaw's Captain Shotover, another former mariner who becomes the spiritual adviser to a young woman and helps to free her from the snares of romantic and sentimental illusion. But the strongest outline discernible behind the lineaments of Josephine Leslie's novel belongs to the genre of "New Woman" fiction, a category of feminist writing that flourished in the 1880s and 1890s and, as Ann Ardis rightly has suggested, "did not end at the end of the nineteenth century" (Ardis, 168).

Leslie begins her narrative not in the contemporary world of the mid-1940s, but in an unspecified moment around the turn of the century, at a time when automobiles are already common, yet the only respectable employment that Lucy's middle-class in-laws can imagine for her is still in "hat shops or tea shops" (3). It is a time when the battle for a woman's right "'to be left alone to live my life as I wish and not as other people think best for themselves'" (58), as Lucy puts it, must be waged unceasingly, against great opposition. The arguments that Lucy's sister-in-law, Eva, uses against her are familiar ones from the "New Woman" literature of the Nineties, hurled against earlier heroines such as Herminia Barton of *The Woman Who Did* (1895) by Grant Allen, Bridget Ruan of *Nobody's Fault* (1896) by Netta Syrett, Mary Desmond of *The Wheel of God* (1898) by "George Egerton" (Mary Chavelita Dunne), and Cosima Chudleigh of *A Writer of Books* (1898) by "George Paston" (Emily Morse Symonds). She accuses Lucy of having lost her femininity: "'Really, Lucy, I can't think what has happened to you lately,' said Eva. 'You used to be such a sweet little thing'" (58); she accuses her of suffering from "hysteria," when Lucy begins laughing in her presence, and threatens to take her "to a doctor the first thing in the morning" (59); and, above all, she accuses Lucy of having become "selfish." The marks of this grave feminine sin include everything from Lucy's early insistence upon having a room of her own, rather than sharing one with her young children ("'[A]nd wasn't it rather selfish of dear little Lucy to have chosen the best room in the house for her own bedroom? That should be the schoolroom'" [53], Eva declares) to her refusal years later to force Anna, her daughter, to give up a career as a dancer so as to please Cyril, her priggish son. As in the "New Woman" fiction which Leslie's novel deliberately recalls, patriarchy polices the life of the heroine through her nearest relations, both female and male, enforcing the code of "selflessness" and also attempting to set mothers and daughters against each other, to preclude the possibility of their combined rebellion. But again, as in some of those earlier models of feminist writing, such as the short stories "Virgin Soil" (1894) by "George Egerton" or "For Better, For Worse" (1897) by "George Fleming" (Julia Constance

Fletcher), mothers and daughters who have been made to view each other as rivals or as obstacles learn to support one another's best interests. At the same time, these earlier narratives, many of which feature protagonists who turn into artists or writers, give Leslie an example of how to expose "the tensions between women's desires and aspirations, and the . . . gender system in both its ideological and social and material forms" (Pykett, 142).

In terms of narrative design, invoking the ghost of the "New Woman" novel and using it as her ally enables Leslie to avoid the marriage-centered structure that dominated popular women's fiction of her own day. The scope of *The Ghost and Mrs. Muir* is broad, opening with Lucy's first moves toward independence after she has become a widow and concluding with her death many decades later; indeed, it even continues beyond that moment of death, with which a less adventurous work might have ended, to depict Lucy's own transmutation into ghostly shape. Along the way, Leslie's novel is constructed episodically as a series of events that test Lucy's resolve first to live for herself and, later, to live by herself. Of these, the romantic interlude with Miles Blane is merely one in a succession of dangers to be overcome, not the focus of the plot—though, significantly enough, Joseph Mankiewicz's 1947 Hollywood adaptation turns it into the chief incident of Lucy's life. Equally important, nonetheless, in Leslie's original version are such challenges as Eva's interfering visit to Gull Cottage, and, in the latter half of the novel, the separate efforts of Lucy's son Cyril and of her daughter Anna to make their mother leave her own house and move in with one of them. Resisting each of these forms of loving coercion proves as difficult, in its own way, as casting off her desire to be with the perfidious Miles Blane. On each occasion, Lucy must struggle against the social ideology she has internalized, which leads her to believe that pleasing others is woman's highest duty. At one point, Lucy asks in despair of the wise ghost at Gull Cottage whom she has made her preferred adviser, "'Must growing up always mean a breaking up?'" to which the answer that comes back is "'No, but it often means a breaking away'" (107). Certainly, there is a parallel between the "breaking away" that the protagonist must accomplish, over and over again, in the course of the narrative and the "breaking away" that the text itself achieves, as it finds its substitutes for the expected romance plot in narrative forms both conventional and unconventional—the resurrected "New Woman" novel, which charts the quest for female selfhood in a middle-class context, and the comic-gothic novel, which faces down anxiety about the unknown with laughter.

In *Comic Effects: Interdisciplinary Approaches to Humor in Literature,* Paul Lewis has identified four broad patterns to describe the different ways in which humor can operate within gothic literature. The first of these, according to Lewis, "in which the fear stimulated by incongruity is overwhelmed by humor, is typical of mock-Gothic works in which extreme mystery and fear are repudiated and fantasies of horror are laughed out of mind" (116); the third, "in which the response to mystery is an unsettled combination of humor and fear, appeals to writers using an emotional indefiniteness or ambiguity to expose the limits of value systems" (116). Both of these categories seem to apply to Leslie's *The Ghost and Mrs. Muir;* yet because it is not only a gothic comedy, but a feminist comedy with social pronouncements to make, it also draws upon strategies that fall outside of Lewis's account. One of these is a technique of reversal or substitution, in which gothic disruptions of domestic life that ordinarily might produce fear instead prove laughable, but in which the everyday situations of domestic life reveal themselves as terrifying and threatening to the female protagonist. Through such reversals, the text redefines the sources of psychic peril for women. It is not the supernatural with which they must do battle, but the so-called "natural" sphere of social responsibilities and demands. So overwhelming to the protagonist, in fact, is the "mystery" of how to survive amid the competing and confusing expectations of others, that she can do so only with help from the immaterial world.

Like Oscar Wilde's short story, "The Canterville Ghost" (1887), before it, Leslie's novel conjures up an essentially moral spectre, who only plays his fearsome practical jokes upon the unworthy and who establishes a bond of sympathy with the heroine. Leslie takes the relationship between her ghost and heroine one step beyond, however, to suggest that the supernatural jests may in fact be projections of the female protagonist's own otherwise inexpressible frustrations. Capt. Daniel Gregg delights in chasing from his house the estate agent who attempts to make up Lucy's mind for her, in pushing the meddling Eva into a stream and blasting cold draughts upon her indoors, and in shaking up a dinner party filled with hypocrites and smug clergymen by producing a "curious booming sound . . . and a rush of air . . . blowing out the tall candles on the dinner table, [and] slamming the door in the face of the butler, who was bringing in the port" (142), so that Lucy has an excuse to simulate fainting and escape their company. The ghost's actions toward the protagonist are, in fact, almost wholly benevolent and protective. His first material apparition before her eyes, right after she has had a dream in which his painted portrait comes to life, follows his effort to save her from accidental asphyxiation from gas fumes by unlatching a window. Immediately, this situation which contains the potential for gothic horrors—a woman alone in her bedroom with a male spectre who still has physical powers and can move objects at will—resolves itself into the comedy of an ordinary domestic squabble between two teasing partners:

> "Oh, so it was you that opened the window and nearly froze me to death," said Lucy.
>
> "You exaggerate like all women," said Captain Gregg. "The fresh air was good for you, and it merely made your nose a little red."
>
> "It didn't," said Lucy, and suddenly began to laugh.
>
> "What's the joke?" asked Captain Gregg. "I like a good laugh myself, and God knows this house has heard little enough of laughter in these last twelve years."
>
> "It seems too ridiculous that I should be arguing with a ghost over a red nose," said Lucy. "Such a music hall thing to do, I mean—and before supper I was terrified of you, scared nearly to death."
>
> "We are always afraid of the unknown," said Captain Gregg. (31–2)

What *The Ghost and Mrs. Muir* attempts, nevertheless, to teach the female reader is to throw off caution and embrace the creative energy of the unknown. According to the novel's variation upon the gothic formula, the unknown should be seen as the realm of women's greatest possibilities; it is the known that ought to be distrusted and even dreaded, for that is the sphere in which women have been and continue to be subject to limitations, deceptions, injustices, and abuse. Lucy is always safest in her haunted house and in the company of its rather eccentric resident ghost, while in the mundane world of close and distant relatives, clerics, and titled authorities, on the contrary, she is most at risk. Just as Josephine Leslie domesticates the unfamiliar through comedy, so she exposes the sinister aspect of the domestic and the familiar by withholding laughter. The one episode in the novel that arouses true gothic emotions, either in the heroine or in the reader, involves nothing more mysterious than dinner at the house of the Bishop, whose daughter is about to marry Lucy's son, Cyril. As the assembled guests offer ill-informed and offensive comments upon a current best-seller—which, unbeknownst to them, was written by Lucy Muir herself with the help of her "ghost"—Lucy experiences both the terror that stems from fear of discovery and the suffering that comes from her helplessness in the face of insult and injury: "Seated at the Bishop's right . . . she felt so frozen with horror at the situation she found herself in that she was past blushing and beyond speech" (139). Under the weight of these gothic perceptions, her only immediate recourse is to draw upon the gothic convention for a heroine in peril—that is, to faint. Even in using that convention, however, she revises it, for unlike the usual heroine of such narratives, she expresses the need not merely to escape *from* danger, but to escape *to* the delights of communion with the self, with the imagination freed by solitude. As Lucy explains about her gesture of fainting to the ghost, who appears the moment she is alone again, "'I had to do something in order to be by myself and talk to you'" (144).

But talking with a ghost is not purely an exercise in solipsism. Out of these conversations with the supernatural comes a tangible product of real benefit to others—the book called *Blood and Swash,* ostensibly the story of Captain Gregg's life and adventures—which evolves through circumstances that play humorously upon the notion of "ghostwriting." Lucy chooses to tell herself that it is the spectre haunting her house who pushes her, "by bullying and persuasion" (124), into producing the manuscript; yet it is actually her own conviction of "the very real need for the money the book might bring" (124) and her determination to earn that herself which carries her through "night after night, keeping her up till all hours, tapping away at the typewriter" (124).

Rearranging Gull Cottage into an artifact that pleases her and ordering her own life to suit herself may be Lucy's preferred art forms, her vehicles for self-expression, but they do not pay. Although she may learn in the first half of the novel how to be emotionally self-sustaining, Lucy must still confront the problem of how to earn money. Indeed, the education that she receives through the course of the narrative is in part an economic one. As she muses aloud to her ghostly companion,

> "Isn't it amazing," she went on, "the power that money has? I'm only just beginning to realize it. If you know you are secure and well dressed, and there will always be taxis to take you out of the rain, and maids to scrub the floors, and cooks to prepare your meals, you somehow feel the world is your oyster with a fine pearl in it—poverty is no disgrace, but it can make one feel as if one were born in a dustbin . . . ." (164)

At the very moment when Josephine Leslie's female readers were being encouraged by political and social authorities in England to surrender their roles as wage-earners and to entrust themselves to the care of the men returning from the front, *The Ghost and Mrs. Muir* emphasizes, both through the protagonist's situation and through her reflections upon it, the importance for a woman of having an income of her own, completely separate from her husband's. Lucy argues this point explicitly with her grown daughter, Anna, when the latter announces her engagement to a rich man. For Anna, the marriage is not only a welcome opportunity to give up her career onstage as a dancer, but a reason to accept no further money from her mother; "'And when I am married you won't have to give me an allowance,'" she declares (162). But Lucy sees matters more pragmatically: "'Oh, yes, I will,' said Lucy, 'you don't know how humiliating it is to have to ask even for a penny to buy a stamp. I had no money when I first married and I know what that is like'" (162).

Lucy's earliest articulation of the importance of earning money of her own results from her concern for others: "And though Cyril had won a scholarship, he needed money for clothes and books; indeed he seemed to need more and more money, and there were Anna's expenses to be paid as well. And then Cyril fell ill, and the doctor said that an operation for appendicitis was necessary"(109). But she quickly moves on from such socially approved feminine selflessness to more self-interested matters—namely, anxiety over the possibility of having to give up Gull Cottage, that tangible representation of her aesthetic, philosophical, and emotional liberation and autonomy. With the aid of her ghost, who supposedly "dictates" to her the history of his career as both a sea captain and a sexually active man, Lucy writes a book intended from the start to be nothing more than a money-making venture, designed to let her keep her house. Yet what she discovers in the course of its production is that conventional snobbish distinctions between "popular" literature and "good" literature are as arid and suffocating as all the other cultural taboos from which she has gradually been freeing herself at Gull Cottage. *Blood and Swash,* as this allegedly collaborative work is called, is, like *The Ghost and Mrs. Muir* itself, both a sensational story and an instructive one; its lessons for the audience are inseparable from the thrills and the laughter it inspires. Clearly, Josephine Leslie means Capt. Gregg's modest defense of this undervalued genre to echo beyond the text: "'Is this book wisdom?' asked Lucy, putting the manuscript back on the table. 'It has some elements of wisdom in it, me dear,' replied the captain" (129).

While the composition of *Blood and Swash* provides an occasion for challenging the reader's belief in literary hierarchies, the physical preparation of the manuscript also becomes an unanticipated opportunity for increasing the protagonist's own sense of mastery and self-sufficiency. In gradually teaching herself to use a typewriter—"This innocent looking little machine [which] seemed to have a perverse personality of its own, that persisted in showering the paper with uncalled-for exclamation marks, with brackets, per-cent signs, fractions and dashes" (121)—Lucy learns not to fear yet another realm of the "unknown," the resources of technology. That the language with which Josephine Leslie describes the typewriter—"innocent" and "little," yet with a "perverse" self-will—also applies so well to the heroine herself, suggests how completely the act of sitting down to write and of confronting the typewriter parallels a woman's exploration into her own refractory and lawless consciousness, into the realm of the "uncalled-for."

When the narrative persona of "Professions for Women," Virginia Woolf's 1931 lecture to the Women's Service League, prepared to write, she, too, found herself face-to-face with the "uncalled-for" in the form of a ghost:

> I discovered that if I were going to review books I should need to do battle with a certain phantom. And the phantom was a woman, and when I came to know her better I called her after the heroine of a famous poem, The Angel in the House. It was she who used to come between me and my paper when I was writing reviews . . . . The shadow of her wings fell on my page; I heard the rustling of her skirts in the room. (Woolf, "Professions," 236–7)

Woolf's would-be collaborator, however, proved herself traitorous and obstructive at every turn, as she "made as if to guide my pen" (237). Insisting that women must maintain the illusion of modesty and "purity," even in their writing, this phantom censored not only "the truth about human relations, morality, sex" (238), but all forthright or controversial statements, in favor of a language of euphemism and evasion, in favor of "charm." To preserve the integrity of her literary vision from such interference, Woolf's persona was forced to deal violently with this spirit haunting her subconscious: "I turned upon her and caught her by the throat . . . . Had I not killed her she would have killed me. She would have plucked the heart out of my writing" (237–38). But this phantom was, according to Virginia Woolf, more than merely a personal demon; "Professions for Women" identifies her as the cultural plague of every middle-class female author of Woolf's generation, so that "Killing the Angel in the House was part of the occupation of a woman writer" (238).

For Leslie's Lucy Muir, too, becoming a professional writer means struggling with a spectral presence that attempts to seize control of her text. But the dialogues in *The Ghost and Mrs. Muir* reverse Woolf's formulation of the problem for women authors. It is Lucy herself who functions, at least at first, as the mouthpiece for the sorts of aesthetic and cultural proprieties dear to the Angel of the House, whereas it is the seemingly alien spirit invading her room and her mind who impatiently dismisses all standards except those of accuracy and plain-speaking. In their comical sparring matches, which are always far more affectionate in tone than Woolf's murderous confrontation with her female nemesis, Lucy and the Captain in the House battle over issues small and large, involving both language and content. Each time that Lucy attempts to censor either an expression or a thought, the ghost challenges her not to shrink from it. During their collaborative writing, for instance, of the chapter describing Captain Gregg's sexual misadventure in Marseille, the ghost responds to her hesitation over a phrase by snapping, "'Brothel,' said the captain, 'don't mince words, Lucia. If there's a good old English word, use it'" (122), just as he insists that she overcome her distaste for narrating the episode at all by reminding her, "'And these things do happen and far worse, and they'll happen again to other young fellows in foreign ports unless they are warned'" (122). If Woolf's angelic phantom was the embodiment of culturally mandated repression, internalized by the middle-class woman writer who has been raised to be ladylike, Josephine Leslie's bumptious ghost is the opposite—a personified projection of the boldness and openness that a "respectable" woman writer of Lucy Muir's class longs to experience. In the opportunities that he presents to the female imagination for vicarious adventure, Captain Gregg has less in common with the "Angel in the House" than with another of Virginia Woolf's creations: the title character of her comic novel *Orlando: A Biography* (1928), through whom Woolf lives out the fictional life of a dashing Elizabethan courtier-warrior-poet and lover of women.

Thus, according to Leslie's text, the process of self-discovery that a twentieth-century woman must undergo in order to write can be more positive and uplifting than Woolf had suggested—not merely a matter of wrestling with an Angel, but of becoming the Captain of one's soul. Yet, though far different from the homicidal scene of Virginia Woolf's imaginings, such an encounter still carries the potential for painful repercussions of its own. Over and over, Lucy's Captain forces her to apply to her life the same standards of rigorous truth-telling that she learns to bring to writing. Through the borrowed vision of this man-of-the-world, through the eyes of the ghost in her house, Lucy can see clearly, for instance, the impossibility of continuing her relationship with Miles Blane. In the 1947 Hollywood film adaptation of *The Ghost and Mrs. Muir,* the heroine discovers the true character of her lover only by accident, when she unexpectedly meets the wife whose existence Miles has kept concealed. But in Josephine Leslie's original narrative, it is Lucy Muir herself, under the tutelage of her Captain, who recognizes and admits that Miles—with his adolescent impulse to dabble and experiment with women, moving from one infatuation to the next and committing himself wholeheartedly to no one—is hopelessly second-rate. "'Miles doesn't want a wife,'" the "voice" within her consciousness tells her plainly, "'all he wants is a mother and a mistress'"(94), neither of which would or should be an acceptable role for her. Just as the ghost defends the integrity of the text of *Blood and Swash* from Lucy's socially conditioned urge to water down its uglier lessons, so he demands that she not dilute the integrity of her own personality by making compromises with the truth, even about those whom she loves. He compels her to acknowledge the dullness of her late husband, the manipulativeness of her sister-in-law, and the fatuousness and pomposity of her beloved son, who greets the news that she is preparing a manuscript by saying, "'Dear little mother,' went on Cyril sentimentally, 'working away so hard to make money for me . . . .but don't count too much on getting your book published—I mean so many women are writing books nowadays'"(126). Most of all, however, the ghost insists that she laugh at those around her and enjoy the jokes he stages at their expense.

In order to laugh along with the Captain, a woman reader must first expunge from her mind that feminine training in countenancing the vices and indulging the frailties of others which makes most social relations, and certainly most loves, possible. Laughing with the Captain may even mean, as it does for Lucy, choosing ultimately to withdraw altogether from ties to friends and family. Such a position would have been difficult indeed to maintain in 1945, when the British government was making the reorientation of women to domestic life a national priority. More problematic still, however, for Josephine Leslie's female audience today is that to laugh with the Captain is to adopt as one's standard of value what seems to be a masculine point of view. In a text where the embodiment of the comic spirit is also a male spirit, can there be such a thing as feminist humor? Is Josephine Leslie's decision to clothe the principles of freedom, creativity, and wit in male guise yet another example of patriarchal thinking and covert misogyny? And must a woman detach herself from the oppressive institutions of romantic love and domestic ideology only by attaching herself to a man, whether actual or imaginary, who has achieved critical distance from these?

That Leslie herself was similarly troubled by such questions may explain why in a subsequent work by "R. A. Dick," the 1954 novel called *Unpainted*

Portrait, male characters occupy only marginal roles. In that text, the central relationship occurs between two lifelong women friends—one of them a professional portrait artist, the other first an actress and later a nun who retreats to an all-female community—who do not need to use men, either in ghostly or corporeal form, as their muses. Each manages to escape the constraints of social expectations for women without relying upon the guidance of a male wraith. Significantly enough, though, there is relatively little humor in that narrative, beyond one scene in the opening chapter where the narrator discovers the other girl's talents as "an astonishing mimic," capable of performing malicious send-ups of their schoolmates and teachers (Leslie, *Unpainted Portrait,* 10–11). In the absence of a masculine persona through which to express the comic impulse, the impulse itself seems almost to disappear.

Yet, despite Lucy Muir's apparent reluctance to make jokes except through the "voice" of the Captain, flashes of true feminist comedy do manage to show themselves in the *The Ghost and Mrs. Muir.* One such moment arises out of the issue of Lucy's authorship of *Blood and Swash,* which is published anonymously and becomes a tremendous success, except in the stuffy and censorious circles frequented by Lucy's son. Cyril, who has no idea of his mother's connection to the book, has grown up to be a bigoted young clergyman, unable to forgive his sister for disobeying his wishes and pursuing her vocation as a dancer. Late in the narrative, Lucy describes to her daughter the details of Cyril's wedding, including the gifts that she presented to the bride and groom:

> "I gave Celia a pearl ring."
>
> "The one like a bloated teardrop that Granny left you?" asked Anna with interest.
>
> "I had it reset," said Lucy, "and I gave Cyril a cheque for the honeymoon," and suddenly the realization struck her that Cyril was taking his bride to Rome on the first royalties from *Blood and Swash* and she began to laugh. If only he knew! But she could never tell him. (156)

The joke that she plays, almost unconsciously, upon her son has the finest qualities of subversive female humor: it undermines patriarchal standards of propriety and impropriety, yet it causes the object of the joke no pain. In this, it differs from the kind of comedy that Lucy identifies with her late husband's tastes: "'Edwin only laughed out loud when other people were hurt, I mean, if they slipped on a banana skin or sat down on a chair that wasn't there'" (163–4). It remains, too, the female trickster's own secret, shared only with the reader of the text. And Lucy accomplishes this jest, moreover, without the aid or the instigation of her ghost, which suggests that reliance upon a masculine model for how to laugh is a crutch that women comic writers eventually will cast aside, in a future beyond the text.

Casting aside, stripping away, doing without—these are, in fact, the disciplines that Lucy learns over the course of the narrative, beginning with the simultaneous "unveiling" of both the house and of herself and continuing through a long process of emotional divestment. They are the preparation for the final shedding of the known—the sloughing off of her body, "'as a snake sloughs the old skin for which it has no more use'"(174)—that must precede entry into the ultimate realm of the unknown. At the end of her life, the protagonist can contemplate without regret how "one by one all . . . [her] contemporaries were passing away, dropping from the tree of life like autumn leaves; but Lucy had never been dependent on society for happiness, and now she seemed to need it less than ever" (165). Indeed, the only company she requires is that of the ghost, whom she still uses as a comic sparring partner to keep her own wit keen.

Though such a position may have constituted dangerously radical thinking for its day, Josephine Leslie was hardly the only British woman novelist of the postwar period to assert that "marriage . . . stunts mental and spiritual growth" and that "the single state, though characterised by loneliness and a yearning for human warmth" represents "hope" (Baker, 174). Unlike some of those other contemporaries, however, whom Niamh Baker cites as possessing similar views—writers such as Kate O'Brien and Elizabeth Taylor—Leslie carried her message beyond the limited audience for genteel and serious fiction, into the ranks of the vast female public eager for gothic romance and comic tales. In *The Ghost and Mrs. Muir,* she offered her readers the female equivalent of *Blood and Swash*—a sensational book, yet also a wise one. Thus, as the Second World War drew to an end, political circumstances may have pushed the middle-class Englishwomen back into the house; but with a laughing ghost and a feminist heroine to haunt it, extolling the joys of creativity, fearlessness, and emotional self-sufficiency for women, that house would never be the same.

CHAPTER FOUR

The Slim, Fasting Smile: Anita Brookner and Post-Holocaust Women's Comedy

In 1877 the English novelist George Meredith delivered a lecture titled "On the Idea of Comedy and the Uses of the Comic Spirit." When published later that year as *An Essay on Comedy,* it would become one of the classic treatises on literary laughter and would engender a theory with which comic fiction writers still reckon more than a century later. At the center of Meredith's talk was a definition of the spirit of comedy—a spirit different from that of satire, which he depicted as violent and derisive, "working on a storage of bile," and different from that of humor, which he saw as genial and sentimental (Meredith, 44). For Meredith, comedy could best be summed up by the image of a face hovering just above the field of human activities. The face is "luminous and watchful . . . [and marked by] half-closed lips drawn in an idle wariness of half-tension" (47). That tension comes from its state of vigilance, rather than from any ambivalence about its purpose, and especially from its readiness to move immediately into action whenever it discerns follies, pretensions, hypocrisies, or self-delusions. It watches calmly, "as if . . . having leisure to dart on its chosen morsels, without any fluttering eagerness" (48). When it finds such "morsels," it regards its prey with a "slim feasting smile, shaped like the long-bow"(47). It shows no scruples that might cause it to hesitate to seize upon and to savor the appropriate object—though its tastes are more those of the gourmet, than the gourmand—and it accompanies its feedings with "volleys of silvery laughter" (48).

Meredith's Comic Spirit is, therefore, a consumer of others, a creature of appetites, but of appetites that are balanced, predictable, well-ordered, and guiltless. The genderless Comic Spirit (deliberately cast by the pro-feminist Meredith as an "it," rather than as the expected "he") is a reasonable being, too. Its actions are dependent, as Meredith himself says, upon the notion that "our civilization is founded in common sense (and it is the first condition of sanity to believe it)" (47). And part of being reasonable, it would seem, is to believe that under certain conditions human beings forfeit their human dignity. When they do, it is their proper fate to be enjoyed unreservedly by the superior consciousness of the writer who embodies the Comic Spirit and to be made available for the delectation of the writer's audience, as well. Under those circumstances, the Comic Spirit rightfully looms above and selects its victims, rather like the hyper-intelligent Martian presences of H. G. Wells's 1898 moral fantasy *The War of the Worlds,* who are "heads—merely heads" (141), "absolutely without sex" (142), that produce a "sustained and cheerful hooting" (152), as they feed eagerly upon Wells's smug, complacent, and foolish Victorian contemporaries. Indeed, it is tempting to see this aspect of Wells's allegory about the Fall of the British Empire through self-satisfied pride as a specific response to and as the dark reverse of George Meredith's sunny image: a recognition of the horror that one might feel at being feasted upon, whether one has deserved such punishment or not.

The principles articulated in *An Essay on Comedy* have continued to exert their influence upon late-twentieth-century British novelists, both among those who have adopted and adapted the image of the consuming Comic Spirit and among those who have engaged with it in order ultimately to resist it. Into this second category falls Anita Brookner, the art historian and writer of fiction who has published two dozen books, including some twenty or so novels, in England and America. That there would be recognizable traces of George Meredith's theories in her works is hardly surprising, given the debt to her Victorian predecessors that Brookner has acknowledged repeatedly in published conversations with John Haffenden in his *Novelists in Interview* (1985), with Shusha Guppy in the *Paris Review* (1987), and with Olga Kenyon in *Women Writers Talk* (1989). She has, in particular, publicly credited her "grounding in the nineteenth century novel" with what Shusha Guppy has called the "great moral rectitude" of her narratives (Guppy, 158), and she has praised the Victorians for understanding the implacability of moral choice. As Brookner puts this, in answer to one of Olga Kenyon's questions, "[The] nineteenth century was more realistic. You can do this *or* that [Brookner's own emphasis], not an unlimited number of things," a fact that she sees her literary contemporaries in England attempting misguidedly to ignore (Kenyon, 20–21).

Among Brookner's fictional characters are numerous creatures of appetite who resemble and even explicitly recall the nineteenth-century Comic Spirit in their eagerness to find pleasure by feasting upon the perceived absurdities of those around them, and who do not doubt the justice of devouring others as their rightful morsels. They are characters such as Alix Fraser of *Look at Me* (1983)—foils to the protagonists, rather than central figures. Unlike Meredith's personification of comedy, they are gendered as male or female; but like the Comic Spirit, they are defined by their laughter and by the characteristics of their mouths:

> [W]e heard that laughter outside our door, presaging our introduction to Alix . . . [who] had such an aura of power that she claimed one's entire attention . . . . [Her] magnificent mouth opened in one of those laughs that I came to know so well. The mouth, and everything about it, was her most important feature: the long thin lips, the flawless teeth . . . . The brilliance of that laughing face, with . . . the rapacious teeth . . . indicat[ed] . . . immense reserves of appetite and pleasure. (*Look at Me,* 47)

Yet the protagonists of Brookner's novels—some of whom are, in fact, not only authors by profession but, like Frances Hinton of *Look at Me,* writers of comic fiction in particular—have no appetite themselves. They hunger, but they cannot eat; they crave nourishment, but do not enjoy the act of consumption; what they swallow, they fail to digest. Again and again, Brookner proves herself the portraitist of disordered eaters: of male and female characters whose capacity both for intake and for the act of "taking" in general has mysteriously been diminished, and with it, the capacity for taking pleasure. Reduced, attenuated figures, they exist not like Meredith's Comic Spirit, as predatory smiles, but rather as wide, staring eyes and as the disembodied fingers that merely record what is seen. Over the course of the narratives, they become wraithlike witnesses. Something has happened, not only to prevent these protagonists from assuming their expected role as feasters, but to jeopardize their physical survival. As Brookner's comic novelist-character, Frances Hinton, notes unsparingly of herself, while her housekeeper plies her in vain with food:

> Nancy . . . scolded me for having got so thin. I had not noticed it until this morning, but now that she mentioned it I could feel the angular bones of my shoulders and my skirt was slightly loose around my waist. I did not mind. It seemed to me appropriate that I should dwindle, that I should shed my biological characteristics. In future I would become subsumed into my head, and into my hand, my writing hand. (*Look at Me,* 179)

No such fate, however, of physical diminution and annihilation has been decreed for the protagonists from birth. Somewhere, barely recoverable by memory, is the troubling, alternative image of a different possibility, of a child's full body and sated appetite. This is the picture that haunts Fibich, the middle-aged, melancholy hero of Brookner's *Latecomers* (1988). Indeed, it is almost all that remains to Fibich of his past in Germany, from which he had fled alone to England in the 1930s as a young refugee:

> He had . . . an image of himself as a very small, very plump boy, engulfed in a large wing chair . . . feeling lazy, replete, and secure . . . .
>
> But he knew that he could not have invented this image, which returned to him quite clearly from time to time. The fact that he saw himself as fat was crucial, since for all of his adult life he had been laughably, cadaverously thin. For as long as he could remember his mind had been occupied with thoughts of food, of which there never seemed to be enough . . . . He was never to be fully secure in the knowledge that there would be another meal . . . . (*Latecomers,* 31–2)

Although (unlike Frances Hinton) Fibich allows himself to eat, he finds nonetheless that whatever he consumes fails to nourish him or to restore him to his remembered shape and identity. Instead, the awareness of possessing a voracious appetite wars continually with his "habit of caution, of self-effacement," posing a dilemma that becomes a source of anxiety and that spoils his digestion (*Latecomers,* 43).

What has gone wrong with Brookner's protagonists? That there is something psychically amiss with these representations of character is a fact that has been much remarked upon by previous commentators. In a 1995 study, for instance, Ann Fisher-Wirth plays upon Kafka's phrase to label Brookner a "Hunger Artist" and to view all her protagonists as embodying an "unappeasable hunger" (Fisher-Wirth, 10). For Fisher-Wirth, who takes her cue from French psychoanalytic criticism, the origins of this Lacanian void or "lack" must be the primal "loss, or betrayal, or absence of the mother" (10). Social, cultural, and historical circumstances fall away, both for Brookner as author and for her fictional surrogates, in an unindividuated and universalized scenario of separation from the maternal that Fisher-Wirth offers by way of explanation:

> But whatever the specific narrative situation, it refers back fundamentally to loss itself, originating in what Julia Kristev and others describe as the double severance between mother and child, the first taking place at birth,

> and the second with the child's entry into the symbolic order. Brookner writes of a lack every human shares, and a mourning without ceasing. (10)

Certainly, the grief in these narratives is palpable. Whether it is, however, an essential or a more historically contingent condition is a point worth exploring, along with the question of how and why such "mourning" often co-exists in Brookner's narratives with effects that are also unexpectedly *comic.*

Like Ann Fisher-Wirth, John Skinner turns to post-Freudian psychoanalytic discourse in accounting for the plights of Brookner's protagonists. To explain the state of melancholy and loss of vitality manifested by *Look at Me*'s Frances Hinton, for instance, Skinner looks to what he calls a "central act of repression in Frances's narrative" (Skinner, 61). In Skinner's view, what has been repressed is rooted in an individual, sexual misadventure—in this case, Frances's clandestine love affair with a married man, an event that she herself refers to as "that time of which I never speak" even while paradoxically revealing much about the episode to the reader (*Look at Me,* 121). According to Skinner, the "repression" of this incident "reproduces a virtual Brookner *topos*—the distressing memory of an earlier erotic experience" (Skinner, 62). Indeed, the subtitle—i.e., *Illusions of Romance*—of Skinner's book-length 1992 study of Brookner's novels suggests how great a store he places in the role of heterosexual disappointments, absorbed by and buried within the consciousnesses of Brookner's female protagonists, as the source of these characters' feelings of grief and their reluctance to eat or to thrive.

But is the memory of individual "erotic experience," or more particularly of women's failed relationships with men, really so singularly important and so central to Brookner's narratives? I would like to suggest that it may be a heterosexist blind to assume as much—an error springing from stereotypes about the conscious and unconscious concerns both of female protagonists and of women novelists (stereotypes with which male characters and authors are less likely to be burdened by critical commentators). To identify the story of an "erotic experience" as the only significant repressed narrative, whether in *Look at Me* or in any of Brookner's other fictions, is to fall into a trap that Brookner herself avoids. For heterosexual romance is merely one of the innumerable sorts of relationships that shape Brookner's novels and that also shape her protagonists. Equally, if not more, important are the networks of connection among *Family and Friends,* to use the title of Brookner's fifth published novel (1985). Of these relationships, none has greater weight than the bond between children and parents—between daughters and their fathers, too, and not, as a purely Lacanian perspective might lead us to expect, only between daughters and mothers.

Brookner's fictions, especially those from the first half of her twenty-year publishing career (that is, through the early 1990s), proffer multi-generational stories of psychic damage. They are accounts of adult children damaged not so much by their own "experiences," erotic or otherwise, or by a primal severance from the maternal body, but by a transmitted set of experiences, which are never talked about directly and seemingly cannot be disclosed. Nevertheless, the effects of these unarticulated memories have been handed down through family lines and have left the next generation suspicious of "feasting" and comfortable only with fasting, desperate for the sense of reason and justice that is associated with the presence of the Comic Spirit, yet terrified of feeding upon others and thus of allying themselves with those who victimize.

There is indeed a "central act of repression," a silence that both encloses and that simultaneously discloses a particular "time of which I never speak" (to use Frances Hinton's phrase), common throughout Anita Brookner's multi-generational fictions. I would argue, however, that its origins lie neither in separation from the maternal nor in heterosexual psycho-dynamics alone, but rather in what some critics have described clumsily as the "foreignness" of her characters within their English settings (see, for example, Sadler, 65). As Shusha Guppy observes, at the beginning of a 1987 interview with Brookner, "[A]ll your heroines have a 'displaced person' quality, and the family backgrounds are very Jewish, even though not explicitly" (Guppy, 149). In response to Guppy's question, "Were you brought up Jewish?" Brookner replies,

> "Yes, very much so . . . . Not that I am a believer, but I would like to be. As for the 'displaced person' aspect, perhaps it is because although I was born and raised here I have never been at home, completely. People say that I am always serious and depressing, but it seems to me that the English are *never* serious—they are flippant, complacent, ineffable, but never serious, which is sometimes maddening." (Guppy, 149–50)

Guppy's next comment appears to stray from the subject that Brookner herself is intent upon exploring: "The foreignness of your heroines is emphasized by the contrast between them and the very solidly English, Protestant men they are attracted to" (150). Ignoring Guppy's lead, Brookner forcefully returns the conversation instead to her central concern, which is not with the problematics of these heterosexual relationships, but with the greater issue of the differences in experience that divide one identity group from another: "I think the contrast is more between damaged people and those who are undamaged" (150). For Brookner, the category of "Jew" leads directly to the subject of "damage."

Something has indeed "damaged" Brookner's English Jews of the 1980s and 1990s and distinguished them forever from their "undamaged" Church of England counterparts. Something has left them unable to feel "at home, completely" in the country of their birth. Something has aligned them with the cause of seriousness, making mere flippancy a distasteful alternative and comedy itself a questionable mode. Something, moreover, has curbed their appetites, whether for food, for pleasure, or for feasting on the absurdities of their fellows in society. Something has forced them into the role of witnesses and recorders. And something has both bound them inextricably to the generations preceding them and rendered problematic the contemplation of reproducing themselves.

> Once a thing is known it can never be unknown. It can only be forgotten. And, in a way that bends time, so long as it is remembered, it will indicate the future. It is wiser, in every circumstance, to forget, to cultivate the art of forgetting. To remember is to face the enemy. The truth lies in remembering. (*Look at Me,* 5)

So begins Brookner's *Look at Me,* its incantatory and elliptical pronouncements about memory serving as a frame for the narrative to follow and recurring at crucial moments, in ways that will link explicitly the act of remembering with the labors of the writer ("And writing is the enemy of forgetfulness, of thoughtlessness. For the writer there is no oblivion. Only endless memory" [*Look at Me,* 84]). But it would be a mistake to see these words as limited in their application merely to the personal and individual—to the past love affairs alone of the character of Frances Hinton. The "thing of which" Brookner's writer-protagonist does not "speak" is also the thing of which Brookner's novels *do* speak, repeatedly and obsessively, both overtly and covertly: that is, the Holocaust and its aftermath. The Holocaust is the trauma that has occasioned Brookner's "central act of repression": the Holocaust as perceived by a woman born in England in 1928, and thus raised in comparative safety, but who has never felt safe because of it; the Holocaust as remembered by someone who grew up conscious both of the suffering of her relations in Poland and of her own tenuous position as a Jew in England;

the Holocaust as fixed in the memory of a writer who saw European Jewish survivors rejected initially by England and other nations and given the ignomious label of "DPs" or "Displaced Persons."

Brookner's protagonists, like their creator, carry with them a history that is personal, but also communal. Certainly, they are burdened with the memory of whatever disappointments, slights, and injustices may have been visited upon them in their own pasts, lived out within the sphere of English social life. As Bryan Cheyette has reminded readers in the Introduction to his 1998 volume, *Contemporary Jewish Writing in Britain and Ireland*, an anthology that includes a brief excerpt from Brookner's novel *Latecomers,* "One should not . . . underestimate the extent to which Jews have been regarded as Other in Britain . . . . Ever since Israel Zangwill refused to be 'shut up in the ghetto,' as he puts it, Jewish writers in Britain have been made to feel distinctly uncomfortable with their Jewishness" (xxxiv). But in Brookner's fictions, the protagonists (like their creator) are also bearers of recollections of things not done to them, yet to those like them—the panic, deprivation, separation, torture, imprisonment, and death visited upon others, upon the "Family and Friends," who could so easily have been themselves. From such a fate, they may have been spared; from the knowledge of it, however, there is no escape. It is a history that is never exhibited, yet never forgotten.

"Did your parents ever talk about their past—or the holocaust?" asks Olga Kenyon in a 1988 interview with Anita Brookner. "No, and I'm grateful for that," Brookner responds (Kenyon, 10). But the intergenerational transmission of such information needs no words and is, in fact, often more potent for its very wordlessness. "To remember is to face the enemy," (*Look at Me,* 5), as Frances Hinton says, and also to be conscious of a world in which enemies are actual, in which cruelty can take murderous forms, and in which stripping someone else of their dignity and feasting upon them is no mere metaphorical exercise of the Comic Spirit. Within such a framework of knowledge, the question becomes one of how to "enjoy" oneself (or others) at all, without reproducing the crimes of one's enemies and saddling oneself with that guilt, above and beyond the guilt already engendered by survival itself. For the writer who is drawn to comedy, as are both Brookner and her protagonist Frances Hinton of *Look at Me,* the specific formal challenge lies in determining how to create a kind of comedy that does not victimize the objects of laughter or turn the comic author into a victimizer.

This is the dilemma confronting Frances Hinton throughout Brookner's 1983 novel. Even as she attempts to write literary comedy, "skating over the surface, jazzing things up, playing for laughs" (*Look at Me,* 90), she is conscious of something "false, out of alignment, not giving a true note" (191), for the "true note" must also have a tragic cast. In a 1985 conversation with John Haffenden, Brookner has said,

> "I learned sad truths quite early, and I never really got out of those coils—that life is a serious and ultimately saddening business.There are moments when you feel free . . . moments when you have hope, but you can't rely on any of these things to see you through." (Haffenden, 62).

The early encounters with "sad truths," the impossibility of feeling free, and the disinclination to rest upon "hope" that haunt Brookner's works recall S. Lillian Kremer's remarks about the shadows that overhang the writings of a figure such as Hana Demetz, born like Brookner in the year 1928 and also "spared the fate" of many European Jews, having "never experienced the ghetto or concentration camp" directly herself (Kremer, 100). According to Kremer, Demetz's literary "response suggests . . . [a] connection to her Jewish family's Holocaust history, culminating in her reflections on 'the family [that] had . . . died of broken hearts, of crushed hopes,'" even though she could not be classified a survivor of the same atrocities (Kremer, 118).

Brookner's example, in fact, allows us to extend the analyses and the conclusions of Helen Epstein's important study, *Children of the Holocaust: Conversations with Sons and Daughters of Survivors* (1979). Epstein's focus in the 1970s was exclusively on the Canadian- and U. S.-born children of those who had lived through internment in concentration camps and then had left Europe after being liberated. Her subjects at the time described repeatedly the sense of bearing an intolerable weight of suffering and sadness passed on to them by their parents: "I felt they had imposed a burden on me," as one young woman put it. Indeed, like their parents, they exhibited from an early age what has been characterized as "Survivor Syndrome":

> Complaints of fatigue, lassitude and feelings of heaviness or emptiness are common. Depressive fatigue is characterized by a feeling of intense unpleasantness and is unrelieved by rest or relaxation . . . . Another important characteristic of such patients is their inability to verbalize the traumatic events. In fact, the experience is of such a nature that it frequently cannot be communicated at all. (Epstein, 104–5)

As young adults, they showed empathetic psychic damage, even though many were the products of households in which virtually no mention of the Holocaust had ever been made.

Through Brookner's fictions, we can recognize more fully the legacy of the Holocaust. That legacy exists not only in the sons and daughters of concentration camp inmates, but in all those who grew up as Jews in supposedly "safe" Christian countries, such as England, during the era of th e Nazi's extermination campaigns. The feeling of profound unease, the suspicion, and the absence of security that overhangs Brookner's narratives is no matter of Lacanian lack, but a historically specific response to a political environment in which Jews in general were not "safe."

That Brookner, in shaping her fictions, is consciously working with such a legacy becomes clear from the specific emotional characteristics with which she invests her protagonists. Among the distinctive features shared by the children of Holocaust survivors, as Helen Epstein noted in 1979, is the sense of premature responsibility, of having especially to be the protectors of their parents. As one young woman admitted to Epstein,

> "My relationship with my parents has always been a serious one . . . . We had to be gentle with our parents. Terrible things had happened, so terrible they didn't want us to know about them. I thought a lot about my parents. It was not as if they were the parents and we were the children. We became the parents sometimes and I didn't like that. I would throw tantrums and rebel against the idea of protecting them, unlike my brother, who was always their protector." (Epstein, 37)

Anita Brookner's novels make it plain that such a dynamic could be just as strong between the generations, when it was not the parents themselves who experienced the atrocities, but rather their relatives, their friends, and their contemporaries. Watching the fates of loved ones in Nazi-occupied Europe from the seeming "safety" of England, the adults became sufferers themselves and exhibited to their children a vulnerability and fragility similar to that of the actual concentration camp survivors.

It is to this situation that Brookner makes her first-person narrator allude obliquely yet unmistakably in *Look at Me.* Seemingly around thirty years old in the early 1980s, and thus born in the postwar period, Frances Hinton nonetheless is aware of the intensity of her aging mother's wish to remain within the safety of their London flat in a "reassuring stone building," where "My mother grew to love the solemn clash of the lift gates, for she felt protected and enclosed by them, and this was a need which grew in her with the years" (24–5). Even after her mother's death, Frances cannot bring herself to move away from this fortress-like environment, with "the gravity of its overall demeanour," despite her own desire to reject the legacy of "that reliance on old patterns, that fidelity, that constancy, and the terror behind all of these things" (30–31). Raised to be the emotional caretaker of parents damaged by an unspecified trauma, Frances frequently expresses her revulsion against that role:

> To me in those days it seemed like freedom not to have to care for anybody's feelings if I didn't want to. I hated every reminder . . . that human beings were vulnerable . . . I had lived with all this for far too long.
>
> I needed to know that not everyone carries a wound and that this wound bleeds intermittently throughout life. (43)

At the same time, she carries within herself an array of wounds. These include an instinct for danger that makes her "alert and wary as an animal" (158) and a sense, when apart from her family and mixing instead with her acquaintances from work (especially with the clearly gentile Nick and Alix Fraser and James Anstey), of being in the presence of those who might at any moment betray her.

Frances Hinton is indeed a victim of the Holocaust, though at several removes from the experience of it. Her destiny is to bear forever the impress of her parents' memories of the helplessness and anxiety that enveloped them as Jews living through World War II in a country that continued to define them as expendable outsiders and "Others," never fully English, never guaranteed protection. About the particulars of this experience, Brookner's novels are always mute. Yet they reveal the unspoken through a language of excess that attaches itself to the domestic sphere and specifically to the reflections of children upon the mystery that surrounds the damaged lives of their parents. Some time after the death of her reclusive and emotionally fragile mother, Anna Durrant of *Fraud* (1992) has a dream in which the unspeakable comes near to being articulated:

> Anna dreamed that she was talking to her mother, who was flushed, animated, and in perfect health . . . . 'How lovely to see you looking so well,' she said to her mother. 'Oh, I was always well in those days,' her mother replied . . . .
>
> Then what happened? Mother, what happened? Waking with a violent shudder, she wanted urgently to confront her mother and ask what had led to her long claustration. But my mother is dead, she thought . . . and we never had this type of conversation. Was she like this before I knew her? And what had she to say to me? (*Fraud,* 107)

But what remains to be said has already been articulated obliquely for the reader earlier in the novel, through Anna's own melodramatic, yet unconsciously appropriate, choice of phrasing: "'I don't believe in living in the past,' she said, thinking back briefly to the holocaust of her mother's clothes and possessions that had taken place in a single day . . ." (33).

Bryan Cheyette has described Anita Brookner as making "overt the silence that surrounds Jewishness within English national culture" through her own deliberate silence about the status of characters who are nonetheless obviously Jews (Cheyette, xli). Brookner, however, has been more explicit outside of her fiction, particularly in her *Paris Review* interview of 1987, in addressing the condition of Jews who grew up in England under the shadow of the Holocaust and who developed prematurely the sense of adult responsibility and moral gravity that Epstein's subjects also describe:

> "I was brought up to look after my parents. My family were Polish Jews and we lived with my grandmother, with uncles and aunts and cousins all around, and I thought everybody lived like that. They were transplanted and fragile people, an unhappy brood, and I felt that I had to protect them . . . . As a result I became an adult too soon and paradoxically never grew up." (Guppy, 149)

Anita Brookner's novels demonstrate repeatedly through the medium of fiction what Tony Kushner has observed in the sphere of social fact: that the effects of the Holocaust were pervasive and ineluctable for all British Jews who either lived through World War II or were raised in its aftermath, irrespective of their distance from the actual sites of horror. As Kushner writes in *The Holocaust and the Liberal Imagination* (1994),

> The Holocaust made a deep impact on British Jewry but this would be largely reflected in an increasingly inward-looking and insecure worldview. Few Jews in Britain . . . would be involved immediately in measures of relief and rescue for the survivors, but practically all would be scarred by the realization of what had occurred, responding with a mixture of fear, insecurity and guilt. (Kushner, 223)

Given these scars upon their psyches, can Anita Brookner's protagonists ever wear the mask of the Comic Spirit upon their faces? Can "fear, insecurity" and, most of all, guilt over having survived—a guilt that manifests itself in a kind of wasting sickness; a reluctance or inability to consume, to thrive, and to bring another generation into the world—be consonant with the mode of "feasting" engaged in by that smiling visage? Over the past fifty-five years or so, comic modes of various registers have played an important role in post-Holocaust discourse in general, whether in literature, popular culture, or in personal life. Helen Epstein, for instance, records in detail the case of a thirty-one-year-old man whom she calls "Yehudah Cohen," the son of a survivor of Auschwitz, who is both proud of and defensive about his penchant for making "incisive, mirthless jokes," including some about his family history:

> "I introduce visitors to my wife, my daughter, and Uncle George," he told me, pausing like a stand-up comedian for me to grasp the setup for his punchline. "Then I point to the nearest lampshade." (Epstein, 239)

When Epstein objects to her subject's remark, saying that "I didn't think his joke was funny," he justifies his own recourse to "gallows humor" by describing the practice as one learned from his father:

> "He never told me horror stories about the war. If my father told any stories at all, they were humorous one. They were jokes. I think the way my father can . . . verbalize only the humorous aspects helped him—not physically, but emotionally—through the camps." (Epstein, 239)

Perhaps it is not surprising that Helen Epstein fails to appreciate the joke. The comic strategy employed by "Yehudah Cohen" and his father is one more commonly associated with masculine preferences in laughter—for a comedy that alienates and creates distance, holding at arm's length both the horror of the experience alluded to and the sympathies of the auditor. In a 1991 research project designed to elicit gender differences in approaches to humor, the psychologist Mary Crawford determined that "Men were higher in hostile humor, jokes, and slapstick comedy," all categories involving the infliction and/or deflection of pain, as well as the circumvention of intimacy (Crawford, 31). Such modes of laughter, like those enjoyed by George Meredith's nineteenth-century-born Comic Spirit, contain within them the potential not merely for exposing cruelty, but for reproducing it, if at a lesser level. In a post-Holocaust context, however, such a potential becomes doubly problematic, as it gestures toward the very sadism and callousness that prefigured indifference to the sufferings of ethnic, religious, and sexual minorities during World War II.

Is an alternative kind of comedy written within the framework of Holocaust-awareness possible? Certainly, differing styles of comedy in general, beyond the "hostile" masculine varieties, already exist. Drawing upon studies in discourse analysis by sociolinguists such as Daniel Maltz and Ruth Borker, Mary Crawford describes a common pattern that has been identified in much comedy by and for women, noting that "Women's humor supports a goal of greater intimacy by being supportive and healing" (Crawford, 32). A "feminine" comedy of post-Holocaust consciousness that encourages identification and empathy, instead of distance is, therefore, easy to imagine. To some extent, that is in fact what Anita Brookner has produced, while shunning comic practices that might wound or diminish the targets of laughter, even those "gentler" strategies sometimes deployed by other women authors. As Brookner has noted with dismay, in a review of Barbara Pym's posthumously published comedy, *An Unsuitable Attachment* (1982), "This was the novel that [Jonathan] Cape rejected in 1963, and one begins to see why .... [There] is an unkindness in it which refuses to show its hand"("Bitter Fruits," 31). "Unkindness," especially of a concealed and furtive sort, is the temptation to which the conscience of a post-Holocaust comic author must not surrender.

In her best-known novel, the Booker Prize-winning *Hotel du Lac* (1984), Anita Brookner includes a masculine personification of the Comic Spirit who preaches a philosophy of unkindness, even as he floats above the action, exposing and feasting upon the follies of others. Like the leisurely and detached figure of George Meredith's imaginings, "Mr. Neville" (whose name rhymes with "Devil") seems always to hover at a height beyond the reach of other characters, even if he is in fact sleeping with them. The reader's first perception of him comes through the eyes of Edith Hope, the novel's protagonist: "Startled, she looked up to see a tall man in a light grey suit smiling down at her" (*Hotel,* 55). A "heartless man" (97), he is distinguished always by his unwavering smile, which remains "controlled and ambiguous" (183). Whenever the guests at the small Swiss hotel indulge in a display of their vanities or pretensions, he can be found "enjoying himself hugely," for, as Edith recognizes, he is "a connoisseur of the fantastic, an intellectual voluptuary of the highest order" (112). Throughout the novel, he holds out to Edith, a writer of romance fiction by profession, the possibility of joining him on his lofty perch as his wife in name only, and thus of disengaging herself from the pain of romantic dreams and desires, while achieving a secure social position as a married woman. Merely by agreeing to shed all "'emotional investment,'" he explains to her, "'one can do whatever one pleases .... One can be as pleasant or as ruthless as one wants ... [and] simply please oneself'" (94–5).

Edith, however, chooses not to be ruthless. Much of the first half of *Hotel du Lac* is made up of letters, which will remain unsent, that she composes for the benefit of her married lover back in England—letters offering comic views of her fellow guests at the hotel in Switzerland. Hers is a particularly harmless form of comic writing, for the women whom she describes with her lightly humorous touch are not known to the intended reader; neither are they ever aware that they are being featured in these letters. In the end, moreover, Edith will destroy the record of this one-sided correspondence. At the same time, too, her seemingly unsympathetic comic writing co-exists with social situations in which Edith devotes much care and attention to listening to the other guests, serving as a sympathetic audience for them, and, when necessary, propping up their egos. There is nothing in her conduct that should generate feelings of guilt or self-doubt. Yet even under these circumstances, Edith cannot maintain the detachment required for such a perspective, nor can she keep from implicating herself in the flaws of the world that she examines from a comic angle. With growing distress, she realizes that

> Unsound elements seemed to have crept into her narrative . . . . to amuse, to divert, to relax—these had been her functions, and indeed her dedicated aim. But something had gone wrong or was slipping out of control. What had been undertaken as an exercise in entertainment . . . had somehow accumulated elements of introspection, of criticism, even of bitterness. (114)

Gradually, she finds that the "barriers of her mind," meant to separate "amusement . . . [from] seriousness and . . . painful reflection," have "eroded" (116), and that depression and despair have begun to flood through her: "And at this very late hour, she felt her heart beat, and her reason, that controlling element, to fragment, as hidden areas, dangerous shoals, erupted into her consciousness" (116). Laughing at other women, even in private, grows insupportable to one who is so aware of the pain of life herself.

The female characters, therefore, who serve at first as the unknowing targets of her secret barbs become, by the end of the narrative, heroic figures in Edith Hope's presentation of them. Chief among these transformed characters is Madame de Bonneuil, who moves from the status of an almost Dickensian object of caricature—a "pug-faced lady" (17), "very small, with . . . legs so bowed that she seemed to throw herself from side to side" (16)—to that of the embodiment of courage and persistence. Elderly, deaf, and practically lame, and all but abandoned by a son who finds her presence too inconvenient in his new household, Madame de Bonneuil carries on uncomplainingly, despite everything. At a climactic moment, indeed, Edith invests this figure with immense dignity through her narration of Mme. Bonneuil's progress through the hotel dining room, supported by other women:

> Edith got up, went over to Mme[.] de Bonneuil, and offered her an arm. A pleased but puzzled smile flickered doubtfully across the latter's face, but at that moment Monica [another guest] . . . strolled out of the bar and called, 'Wait for me!' Mme[.] de Bonneuil, each arm securely tethered, her stick carried by Alain [a hotel employee], proceeded, accompanied by Edith and Monica, into the dining room, her head held high, her expression worldly, her demeanour superior to her surroundings . . . . Mme[.] de Bonneuil pressed both the younger women's hands warmly . . . . [and] throughout dinner her head remained high and from time to time her smile returned. (175–6)

The smile of Madame de Bonneuil has nothing in common with the smile of the Meredithian comic spirit, and the pleasure that it expresses comes at no one's expense. Similarly, the moment that the scene above records is, in technical terms, a comic one, but its comedy bears no relation to the mode that exposes and "feasts upon" the subject's flaws or pretensions. It is instead a comedy of survival, revelling quietly in an individual triumph that has been made possible through the aid of a female community. The human subject here is "enjoyed" for her victory over physical and emotional dissolution, as well as over abandonment and victimization by others. Moving beyond her role as narrator, Edith Hope not only shapes the action in this scene through her description, but participates in it and helps to determine its affirmative outcome.

Both here and throughout the latter half of the novel, Edith refuses the pose of distance from those around her. Instead, smiling along with them rather than at them, she celebrates the women of the "Hotel du Lac" (an obvious pun on "Lack," though in a non-Lacanian sense), regardless of their imperfections or of what may at first look like defects, for their ability to survive.

But precisely what is it that they have survived? What does it mean to come back alive from the "Hotel du Lac," as all these figures—including Monica, a severely depressed woman whose eating disorder interferes with her ability to bear children—will manage by the end to do? Throughout the novel, the Swiss location, the hotel building itself, and the natural landscape surrounding it seem to carry an enormous freight of significance, never quite revealed. These settings are burdened at every turn with an extravagantly excessive language of imagery and emotion that has little to do with the actual narrative, particularly with the rather trivial dilemma of Edith Hope, who has left England temporarily until a recent flap over a broken engagement blows over. Brookner's narrative gestures continually toward something beyond itself. Edith meditates upon her trip by steamer across the middle of the lake (i.e., into the "lac" or the site of "lack," whether the lack of knowledge or the lack of control over her own fate):

> But it seemed to Edith that this journey was too serious to be thought of simply in terms of diversion. The empty lake, the fitful light, the dream-like slowness with which they were covering the distance, seemed to have an allegorical significance. Ships, she knew, were often used by painters as symbols of the soul, sometimes of the soul departing for unknown shores. Of death, in fact. Or, if not death, not of anything very hopeful. Ship of fools, slave ship, shipwreck . . . . Edith, once again, felt unsafe, distressed, unhoused. (159–60)

The nature of the allegorical weight that this novel carries is, I would argue, both spoken and not spoken aloud, simultaneously repressed and revealed, in the course of Edith's reflections. The "ship of fools" is, of course, a figure drawn from the arts of the Renaissance—specifically, from literary satire. Yet it is also, unforgettably, the title of Katherine Anne Porter's 1962 novel and of the internationally publicized 1965 film made from it by Stanley Kramer. Both novel and film function as shipboard allegories for the political climate of pre-Hitlerian Germany and, in particular, as representations of the precarious situation of German Jews returning from abroad to their homeland—or rather to a nation that was about to declare that it would no longer be a home to Jews, whose ultimate destination would be an unforeseen voyage toward death.

In the liminal, seemingly neutral space of Switzerland where *Hotel du Lac* takes place, the narrative atmosphere is dense with the repetition of words signalling expulsion, statelessness, danger, and forced confinement. Readers learn early that Edith's stay there is an "exile" (8; see also 52), necessitated by the fact that "home . . . had become inimical all at once" (8). At the airport, as Edith prepares to leave her English homeland, she is overwhelmed by sensations that would seem to have nothing to do with the act of embarking on a brief holiday: "I should not be here! I am out of place! Milling crowds, children crying . . . . For a moment I panicked" (10). Once having reached the Hotel, she experiences its atmosphere as one of "deadly calm" (17): "As in dreams she felt both despair and a sort of doomed curiosity" while exploring the geographical boundaries of her surroundings (21). On her first walk outdoors, "the path . . . seemed to promise an unfavourable outcome: shock, betrayal, or at the very least a train missed, an important occasion attended in rags, an appearance in the dock on an unknown charge" (21); the last image she employs is a self-consciously Kafka-esque one that subtly links Edith to the famous Eastern European Jewish novelist, at the same time that it recalls the (il)legal persecution of Jews under Nazism. The very shops in the nearby town strike her as "houses of detention" (45). As the self-control on which she prides herself gives way, she begins to fear that her status, which seems more to resemble that of a refugee or "DP" than of a mere vacationer, will be permanent: "And maybe I shall not go home, she thought, her heart breaking with sorrow. And beneath the sorrow she felt vividly unsafe" (117).

The comic twist that Brookner gives to these events lurks in Chapter Nine, where she reveals to the audience the very mundane motivation for Edith's flight to Switzerland. After so much portentous rhetoric leading up to it, the cause turns out to be nothing more than social disapproval by friends and neighbors, following Edith's jilting of her fiance on what was meant to be her wedding day. Readers thus enjoy a laugh at Edith's tendency as a writer toward overstatement, for having couched these anti-climactic circumstances in such melodramatic terms. They also laugh at their own gullibility, for having been suckered into expecting the worst. Here, the reader and the protagonist stand at the same level, neither one superior to the other, while laughter circulates harmlessly and painlessly, creating a sense of relief that there is, after all, nothing so terrible at the root of the situation, despite the signs to the contrary.

At the same time, laughing gently both at Edith and at themselves gives the audience a deeper sense of identification with the protagonist. The comedy of *Hotel du Lac* generates intimacy, rather than distance. Brookner's practice thus mirrors what socio-linguists such as Robin Lakoff and Deborah Tannen have often observed in women's discourse and what cultural theorists have noted of women's humor in general. As Susan Carlson put the matter a decade ago in *Women and Comedy: Rewriting the British Theatrical Tradition* (1991), in all genres, "community is basic to the conception and production of women's comedy" (273).

Brookner's comedy regularly aims at establishing a form of community, or at least of commonality, between fictional protagonists and readers, as though to counteract the dreadful sense of alienation from the culture around them that haunts these protagonists. Because of their identity as Jews (an identity that is always hinted at, even when left unspoken), the characters in these novels never feel wholly at ease in their surroundings, whether in England or in Switzerland of the 1980s. It is only with the audience that they achieve a relationship based on some degree of shared experience.

Readers of *Hotel du Lac* join with the protagonist in fearing the worst, but also unite with her later by laughing at their own paranoia, along with hers, when narrative revelations dispel the earlier anxiety. *Time Revealing Truth* is the name of a painting that Edith Hope mentions at a crucial juncture, but it is also a phrase that sums up Brookner's own methods of constructing comic fiction, through the delay and withholding of information (88). The ominous rhetoric of exile and sequestration proves, in the end, to have been a mere comic exaggeration. Despite signs to the contrary, Edith continues to survive, and the novel itself continues to celebrate that survival.

And yet, the effects of that earlier, quite sinister, rhetoric do not disburse, even after time has revealed the supposed truth. On the contrary, the emotions conjured up by the language of displacement, homelessness, and imminent death have a truth of their own, and they remain potent and active. *Hotel du Lac*'s plot may ultimately be that of a comedy, indeed of a romantic comedy out of popular fiction for women (the kind that Edith Hope, a novelist, writes for a living): in the course of the novel, the protagonist turns aside an eligible suitor, flees to Switzerland and narrowly escapes yet another union with someone who will not make her happy, then returns to the (married) man she loves. But Brookner's novel continually traffics in images of a very different nature that seem almost to have been imported from another narrative, images that center especially on the pain of forced exile.

"With aching throat Edith thought of her little house, shut up and desolate, and to which no one came" (145); later, we are told that "she thought of her little house as if it had existed in another life, another dimension. She thought of it as something to which she might never return" (153). Indeed, her repeated, mournful reflections upon the home from which she appears to have been driven, that former place of security for which she longs, do seem related to another source—specifically, to the Holocaust fiction of such women authors as the Polish novelist and short-story writer, Ida Fink. In volumes that include *A Scrap of Time and Other Stories* (1985; English translation published 1987) and *The Journey* (1990; English translation published 1992), Fink, who was born in 1921, records the experiences of female protagonists who were rounded up from their houses and forcibly interred in Nazi-created ghettos, where they awaited an unknown fate, or who fled their villages and tried to reach safety through long and perilous passages. Mirroring the feelings of displacement, grief, and yearning for home recorded by the heroines of European Holocaust stories by Fink and others, Brookner's Edith Hope becomes the vehicle for reminding readers covertly of this history.

A shadow-narrative or counter-text, therefore, with nothing humorous about it, seems to co-exist alongside Brookner's comic plot in *Hotel du Lac* and in other novels. In a few instances, this second story may be situated overtly within the historical framework of the Holocaust (as it is to a greater extent in *Latecomers* and to a lesser one in *Family and Friends*); but more usually, it links itself to Jewish women's perspectives upon the Holocaust through allusion and imagery alone. Perhaps this female Holocaust story is something that Brookner finds it unsafe to tell directly, for its presence might reinforce for an unsympathetic English Christian reader the "strangeness" and "otherness" of fiction by English Jews and might even limit her novels' marketability. Bryan Cheyette has described Anita Brookner accurately as "On one level . . . a prime example of a mainstream British-Jewish writer who has written out virtually any reference to her Jewishness" (Cheyette, xl). But indirection is a strategy often found among women who lived through the Holocaust, whether as survivors or as observers, and it becomes Brookner's preferred way of giving witness to an experience that must not, under any circumstances, be ignored. Claudia Koonz notes of the women who resisted, yet made it back from the concentration camps alive, that they knew from their socialization as females "how to appear harmless and even obsequious to their enemies while maintaining their inner integrity[,] . . . avoid[ing] calling attention to themselves while preserving an internal set of values" (Koonz, 293). Brookner's narratives thus appear harmless by positioning themselves in the category of "British comic fiction," while communicating to their readers simultaneously, at the level of imagery and figurative language, the story of European Jewish women's suffering and of their tenacity in surviving against the odds.

Of her late mother, a Viennese-born woman who spent her married life in England (during a period that would have corresponded to the War years), Edith Hope says,

> I think of her as my poor mother. As I grow older myself I perceive her sadness, her bewilderment that life had taken such a turn, her loneliness. She bequeathed to me her own cloud of unknowing. She comforted herself, that harsh disappointed woman, by reading love stories, simple romances with happy endings. Perhaps that is why I write them. (104)

Edith's writing, it would seem then, is the legacy of her mother's desires—a mode of familial, rather than purely personal, expression. In fact, the legacy of unspecified grief that Edith bears proves just as much a paternal as a maternal one, for the daughter has also absorbed the pain of her "mild" and "puny" father (48), the "poor little professor," who "had died quite young, in his early fifties" (49). Anita Brookner's portrait of the Hope family is never explicitly that of a group of Jews living in exile in England through the time of the Holocaust, yet it unmistakably recalls S. Lillian Kremer's remarks upon Hana Demetz and her "reflections on 'the family [that] had . . . died of broken hearts, of crushed hopes'" (Kremer, 118). These "Hopes," too, have been "crushed."

Yet Edith is the "Hope" that is not crushed and that endures, for she is the one who comes through smiling—not *at* others, but *with* them, especially with other women. She never feasts, especially upon the vulnerable figures who surround her; instead, she fasts—a moral choice to refuse certain kinds of pleasure and enjoyment. "Her own appetite," as she tells the reader, "was gone, quite gone,"and her withdrawal from hedonistic consumption (whether of food or of her fellow exemplars of "lack" and imperfection) assumes the character of a religious observance, almost an echo of the practices associated with Yom Kippur, the Day of Atonement (29). Evidently, Edith does feel that she must atone for having been the only one in her family to live on, and she will not ensure her own existence, if it means treating the powerless as her prey. She survives, instead, at the edge—just as she repeatedly circles the perimeter of the Swiss lake that signifies death—taking in only enough nourishment to keep going and to keep recording what she sees. She will not succumb to Mr. Neville's/Devil's blandishments to "recognize your own true self-interest" (166) and to hover above like the Meredithian Comic Spirit, free of guilt and powerful, even though the alternative may be to "face a life of exile of one sort or another" (165). Instead, she accepts her place as part of the exiled community of the damaged—those who, like Madame de Bonneuil, carry on with dignity and courage. Brookner's protagonist, a slender and diminished representative of the principle of "Hope," may not thrive, but she will continue. As Edith herself says, invoking the spirit of an earlier woman writer, the poet Stevie Smith, "Not drowning, but waving" (10).

Could this mode of survival comedy—a category, as exemplified by *Hotel du Lac,* not merely of literary "waving," but of *smiling*—be labelled "feminist"? As Lizbeth Goodman has remarked pragmatically, "Whether all women's comedy is 'feminist' is as difficult to determine as whether all women's fiction is 'feminist': in both cultural forms, it depends upon who is doing the defining, and for what purposes" (Goodman, 289). Classifying Anita Brookner's work presents particular difficulties, however, for the novelist has shied away publicly from any identification with feminist projects (see Stetz, "Anita Brookner," 98–101). Certainly, her approach to comedy has little to do with the exercise of "revolutionary power" that Jo Anna Isaak finds in much feminist comic art (Isaak, 14) or with the acts of "subversion" on which Lizbeth Goodman ultimately focuses as the defining characteristics of feminist productions:

> "[Feminist] comedy" is that comedy which purposefully subverts traditional expectations about "what women are" or "should be", and which also subverts the very means of expression and representation by and through which such expectations are conveyed. (Goodman, 289)

Among the most important of the "traditional expectations" that Anita Brookner chooses, on the contrary, to reaffirm is the identification of women with domesticity and with the physical space of the home. Again, though, the insistence throughout her novels upon the centrality of home to her female protagonists is not a historically neutral or essentialist matter, but one that bears the specific impress of the Holocaust experience. For a British Jewish woman who lived through World War II and its aftermath, and who thus shared imaginatively in the plight of those driven from their houses by the Nazis and then forced as stateless refugees or "DPs" to relocate after 1945, the concept of "domesticity" can never be understood through the lens of sexual politics alone. What to a Christian feminist writer such as Fay Weldon in *The Life and Loves of a She-Devil* (1984) may look like a situation of confinement, a mere "dead end," from which comedy must help to free all women (Weldon, 37), appears instead to Brookner as the symbol of what was lost, mourned, and recovered only with the greatest difficulty by Jewish women after the War. For such women indeed the "recovery" (whether of psychic wholeness or of domestic property) would never be complete, however greatly longed for.

Brookner gestures allegorically toward this incompleteness at the end of *Hotel du Lac,* where the comic victory for Edith Hope is only partial. To have been to and back from the place of exile, emptiness, and possible extinction, as Brookner's protagonist has been—a site emblematized by the prison-like hotel at the edge of the death-like lake—is to be altered forever. After such an experience, the certainty of possessing even oneself, let alone one's home, must vanish. Hence, the final words of the novel bear the signs of that change:

> "I should like you to get me a ticket on the next flight to London," she said in a clear voice. "And I should like to send a telegram."
>
> When the requisite form had been found, she sat down at a small glass table in the lobby. "Simmonds, Chiltern Street, London W1," she wrote. "Coming home." But, after a moment, she thought that this was not entirely accurate and, crossing out the words "Coming home," wrote simply, "Returning." (184)

The story of the Holocaust recedes in time. A writer for the *New York Times,* reporting on a conference about "the experience of Jewish displaced persons after World War II," held in January 2000 in Washington, D. C. , has put the matter succinctly: "The survivors' children—who call themselves second generation or, frivolously, 2G—have noted that except in history books, few epic tragedies seem to endure beyond the lives of the victims and perpetrators" (Berger, A11). Anita Brookner's achievement has been to make the emotions associated with these "epic tragedies" live on in domestic comedies, specifically in women's comic fictions that promote a sense of closeness and empathy between the reading audience and the suffering character. In *Latecomers* (1988), Brookner's most explicit statement yet about life in the aftermath of the Holocaust, the narrator explains the indissoluble attachment of one man to another, who was, like the protagonist, sent as a child to England from Germany just before the War: "Only the knowledge that someone else's experience reflected his own reality saved him" (6). In Anita Brookner's hands, comic fiction becomes the reflection of a very particular "reality," though the image in the mirror may sometimes seem to be obscured. When seen, however, it turns out to have a smiling face—not the feasting smile of George Meredith's Comic Spirit, in pursuit of "morsels," but a beneficent smile, in search of a like response from others:

> Hartmann smiled. Such smiles they both had, thought Christine. That was what had bound her to them in the first place, their wonderful smiles, eager in Hartmann's case, tentative, like an English sun, in Fibich's. And from the joyless world of her youth she had retained a nostalgia for joy although she herself was untrained for such emotion, and was awkward with it. (*Latecomers,* 231)

The smile that binds is also the smile that saves. Brookner's characters, though damaged, are not drowning, but smiling.

CHAPTER FIVE

Suniti Namjoshi: Laughing with and at Her "Sisters"

In the 1890s, to laugh and to write comic fiction as a British New Woman meant, by and large, to do so as a white, English-born, either middle or upper-middle-class, Church-of-England-going, and heterosexual feminist. Of course, it was not the case that all New Women authors actually occupied such categories. Some, indeed, were born in Ireland, Scotland, Wales, or were from the many regions around the globe that had been appropriated by the Empire; some were lower-middle-class or working-class; some were Catholics, Dissenters, Jews, or atheists; some were lesbians or bi-sexuals. But those who did not embody the "dominant" identity were expected nonetheless to perform that identity in the sorts of comic voices and perspectives that they adopted—to acknowledge its primacy, to speak to and about its preoccupations, and to address readers who also took for granted its centrality, thus reinforcing it as the norm for feminist writing.

It would be difficult to assert that this expectation for women writers of comedy (or for women writers in general) changed much, until nearly one hundred years later. There were, of course, some writers who succeeded along the way in inhabiting and writing from different points of view and, particularly, in countering heterosexist assumptions about gender. Virginia Woolf famously did so in *Orlando* (1928); Molly Keane less famously did so in her *Devoted Ladies* (1934), a comically catty novel about a lesbian couple published under the pen-name of "M. J. Farrell." In the theatre, the staging in 1958 of Shelagh Delaney's *A Taste of Honey* moved women's comedies out of the middle-class drawing-room and toward the "kitchen sink" of the working classes, through a play written in an under-class voice; Delaney's was a work, moreover, that touched upon questions of alternative sexualities and upon race by giving its heroine a gay male friend and a Black male lover.

But such instances remained exceptions, and they almost never extended to involve women of different races or ethnicities writing for or about themselves. Art that was identified, in particular, as feminist continued to be produced by and for white women. When the change came, it did so at the instigation of women who challenged British feminism from within and from without to recognize that the undifferentiated, supposedly universal, category of "woman" was both oppressive and exclusive. The century-long insistence upon the concept of female unity, in the form of an undifferentiated "sisterhood," had not made for a stronger movement, but merely for one that had left and still was leaving many women on its margins, that often gained the narrowest of victories, and that lost much of the political ground it seemed to win.

Feminist theorists of the 1970s and 1980s began to articulate their recognition of something amiss and to do so in terms that emphasized the need for new ways of acting, as well as of thinking. At the same time, numerous calls for bridge-building, reaching outward, and creating coalitions started to appear. In 1973, Sheila Rowbotham warned in the "Conclusion" to her 1973 socialist polemic, *Woman's Consciousness, Man's World,* that "class and race cut across sexual oppression. A feminist movement which is confined to the specific oppression of women cannot, in isolation, end exploitation and imperialism. We have to keep struggling to go beyond our own situation" (Rowbotham, 123–4). Yet even she constructed her progressive argument for joining hands with working-class men and men of color upon the old premise that "our own situation"—the situation of women—could be encompassed in a phrase that used the singular form. It would take feminists of color, such as Hazel Carby, to explode both that phrasing and the thinking that underpinned it. At the climax of "White Woman Listen!"—her 1982 essay—Carby would state uncompromisingly,

> Black women do not want to be grafted onto "feminism" in a tokenistic manner as colourful diversions to 'real' problems. Feminism has to be transformed if it is to address us. . . . In other words, of white feminists we must ask, what exactly do you mean when you say "WE"?? (Carby, 52)

The shift toward acknowledging diversity, difference, and multiplicity, in terms of who constituted "British women" and thus of what constituted "British feminism," happened at varying rates of speed; so, too, did the organizing of various communities of British women and, as a result of such organizing, the production of new bodies of British feminist art. In editing and publishing their 1994 anthology of work by the Asian Women Writers' Collective, titled *Flaming Spirit*—a volume that included Leena Dhingra's wry comedy of manners about class, race, cultural clashes, and inter-generational misunderstandings, "The Guest"—Rukhsana Ahmad and Rahila Gupta proudly celebrated the tenth anniversary of their collective, which had not come together in London until 1984 (Ahmad and Gupta, vii). For the filmmaker and author Pratibha Parmar, too, significant change did not occur until the mid- and late-1980s. As she reported in her essay "That Moment of Emergence,"

> As one of the founding members of the first black lesbian group in Britain in 1984, it was invigorating finally to find a community of lesbians of color where we could talk about our common experiences of racism and isolation within the white lesbian and feminist community, as well as share cultural similarities and a sense of integration . . . .
>
> It was only in the late 1980s that a rigorous critique of an "identity politics" was initiated, attempting to prioritize or create hierarchies of oppression . . . [for] identities are not fixed in time and space, but what is valuable is the multiplicity of our experiences as lesbians of color, as women and as black people. (Parmar, 380)

According to Heidi Safia Mirza, in *Black British Feminism* (1997), the effects of such shifting thought did not make themselves widely felt in white feminist circles until well into the 1980s, for "the vision of universal sisterhood" remained the "consuming unidirectional project of white (socialist) feminism," even as "racial power within the white feminist production of knowledge about gender relations was never problematized" (Mirza, 9). Meanwhile, in the Introduction to her 1988 anthology of prose and poetry by Black women in Britain, *Sojourn,* Zhana (who uses only one name), described "the continuance of internalization of racism" in Black communities, leading the members of those communities—including those in feminist groups—to turn upon and against one another: "Deep-seated rivalries and dissensions exist between African and Afro-Caribbean women, women of African descent and Asian descent, lesbian Black women and heterosexual Black women, mixed-race and 'totally Black' women, etc, etc" (Zhana, 30). It would be more than a decade later, at the very end of the twentieth century, before young feminist writers of the so-called "Third Wave"—whether in Britain or North America—could take it as a given that "Rooting homophobia out of the movement is as essential as rooting out racism," or that "the movement is made up of women from all points on the sexual spectrum," as well as from many different racial, ethnic, and religious cultures and classes, acknowledging and appreciating their unlikeness, as well as their commonalities (Baumgardner and Richards, 64–5).

Gradually, the idea that a single feminism, rather than a multitude of *feminisms,* could be sufficient for all came to be read as a grave and even offensive misconception, as it tends to be today. With this shift in consciousness in end-of-the-century feminist politics, the notion of sisterhood as an easily attainable ideal increasingly grew to be discredited as a sign of off-putting high-handedness, to say nothing of wilful blindness, within the women's movement. It became, in fact, an assumption both deserving of ridicule and answered with laughter, just as misogynist masculine ideologies had been.

Central to this process, especially in Britain of the 1980s, of holding up feminist culture for inspection and of laughing at its flaws, was the comic work of the Bombay-born expatriate writer, Suniti Namjoshi. In volumes such as *Feminist Fables* (1981), *The Conversations of Cow* (1985), and *The Blue Donkey Fables* (1988), published by feminist presses based in England, Namjoshi both dismantled the prevailing platitudes about "universal sisterhood" and staked out her own right as an Asian lesbian to create art, including comedy, in a white-dominated world. She laid claim, too, to her own version of feminism, against the backdrop of what Najma Kazi has described as the hostility of "Asian men [who] constantly throw at us the accusation that when we protest and take up issues of concern to us as women we are aping white women" (Kazi, 54). At the same time, her comic prose also embodied a phenomenon that Nalini Natarajan has noted as common in "Indian diasporic writing"—that is, the "interrogation of a unified 'Indian' identity" (Natarajan, xvii), for Namjoshi's work required the reader to affirm that being an Indian woman and an Indian lesbian, in particular, mattered. Namjoshi's writing of the 1980s was, in fact, survival comedy. It not only asserted a particular sort of identity and the right of that identity to exist and to flourish, but it focused upon changing radically the British and North American political climate—including the feminist environment—in order to make survival possible for others besides herself.

In one of the few extended critical examinations of Namjoshi's work to appear so far, Diane McGifford has described *The Blue Donkey Fables*—a volume produced during this decade of wrestling with then-current feminism and of struggling toward a new vision of *feminisms*—as a book "promoting . . . reformation." "Namjoshi," she states, "as the blue donkey . . . wants us to reform" (McGifford, 295). Yet McGifford also vitiates the specificity of Namjoshi's political thrust by referring to an "us" that is seemingly as undifferentiated as the discredited essentialist notion of "woman." McGifford claims here that "Through her wise, feminist donkey Namjoshi pokes fun at human pretensions, stupidities, and frailties" (295). In this latter statement, McGifford's language is that of the traditional, apolitical theorist of humor, repeating universalist definitions of what satire does—i. e., addressing faults common to all. "Her wit," McGifford says, "spares few of us. Poets, feminists, literary critics, readers, and patriarchs—Namjoshi, as the blue donkey, castigates all of these, some more severely than others" (295).

But these broad notions of who is being targeted in fact run counter to Namjoshi's quite particular interest in examining how the hierarchies that operate within social and economic class, race, ethicity, religion, sexual orientation, and even age all shape these categories and result in certain kinds of conduct toward others (as well as toward "Others") that must be exposed and derided. Namjoshi's objects of ridicule are not merely "pretensions, stupidities, and frailties"—that is, matters of attitude. Neither are they harmless foibles. They are instead grave matters of conduct: acts of oppression and exploitation, committed by those who have the upper hand, based on their social power and privilege. And some of these injustices, as Namjoshi points out through her comedy, were occurring within the very feminist movement that was still trumpeting "sisterhood" in Britain of the 1980s.

I

During the decades of ideological change and struggle that followed in the wake of feminism's so-called "Second Wave," the ideal of a single, smiling female visage—that Medusa-headed, emblematic Everywoman of Hélène Cixous's imaginings—proved to be as illusory and untenable in actual life as was any version of feminism that ignored the material differences in experience or opportunity among women. If women indeed were different (and if differences mattered), then no woman could laugh on behalf of all women, define another's reason for finding something funny or not, or appropriate another's experience in constructing comedy for her own political purposes. Comedy, like other areas of feminist writing, turned into contested ground in late-twentieth-century Britain. New questions arose around the historically problematic issue of women's laughter. This time, they involved the authority of those who claimed the privilege of creating certain kinds of humor about certain kinds of subjects and situations. Especially controversial were those instances in which white feminists—supposedly impelled by their desire to build bridges and coalitions—asserted the right not only to speak for, but to *laugh* for, Asian and Black women and to use the circumstances of their lives in England as comic material for their own feminist ends.

The result was a series of contretemps. In her Introduction to the 1990 reissue of *The Great Celestial Cow* (1984), Sue Townsend has described one of these—an uproar provoked by her tragi-comic play about women born in India but living in the English Midlands:

> *The Great Celestial Cow* was the cause of much heated debate amongst the (mostly male) Asian community in Leicester. There was resentment because I was a white woman writer. How dare I criticise the Asian family. Yet I watched many of our critics laughing (and sometimes obviously moved) as they watched the play, only to raise their voices in anger during the discussions after the show. (Townsend, iii).

Townsend's way of retrospectively framing the reception of her play was to look for an explanation that would keep the ideal of sisterhood between white women and Indian women intact. Those who objected to *The Great Celestial Cow*—or so she said in a parenthetical aside that underlined, rather than downplayed, her claim—were "mostly male." Their objections were, therefore, not really about race, but about patriarchal privilege. Thus, Townsend could read these complaints merely as proof of the correctness of the argument that she had been making about oppressive family structures and male domination within the South Asian diasporic community in Britain and, furthermore, as proof of the rightness of having a white feminist expose this systematic sexism at last.

Erased from Townsend's picture, however, was the sort of view being articulated simultaneously, in the mid-1980s, by Asian British women such as Sutapa Biswas. In an interview conducted by Yasmin Kureishi and published in 1987, Biswas, a visual artist, illuminated the political concerns behind her depictions in pastels on paper of South Asian women "sitting together, laughing and talking," and in control of their domestic circumstances (Kureishi, 38–9):

> Focusing on the positive aspects of Asian family life in her work, I wondered why Sutapa hadn't touched on the problems. Regarding her own experience she told me, "I've never really felt that oppressed within my family, the only place I've felt oppressed is outside the home. Of course there are many problems within any sort of home life, and I think there are problems within the Asian community, but those problems exist within every culture in society—I think these things have to be dealt with within

> those societies themselves. I don't see it as important to highlight those issues, because on TV that's all you hear about. ["] (39).

What Biswas chose to "highlight" instead, both through her visual representations and through interviews such as that with Kureishi, was the presence of a comic practice, as well as a comic perspective, within the South Asian diasporic populations living in England. Especially important to Biswas was the need to underline that comedy was being used as a tool—consciously, politically, and frequently—by women artists like herself:

> "Humour and the use of satire is instrinsic to much of my work," Sutapa emphasised, and she was keen to stress, that contrary to how Asians are usually portrayed by the media, as having no idea of the real world—we are in fact very much aware of our economic and political situation . . . . And something which Sutapa sees as lacking, when Asian people are portrayed, is their sense of humour. (39)

Why did she feel it so urgent, in the mid-1980s, to communicate this message through her art? Biswas's representations were meant to counter, it would seem, the sorts of assumption that animated a work such as *The Great Celestial Cow.* This was a play generated, as Sue Townsend would inform readers after the fact, by the white playwright's observation of and meditation upon the meaning of Asian women's laughter:

> I started to write *The Great Celestial Cow* after seeing four Asian women laughing in a street in Leicester. They were leaving a factory and were obviously happy to be out in the fresh air for a while until their household duties claimed them.
>
> When I say that I started to "write" the play, I don't mean that I rushed home[,] grabbed a pen [,] and wrote there and then. What I mean is that I started to think about the lives of Asian women in Leicester. (Townsend, iii)

For Townsend, the conduct she had seen signified only the group's spontaneous sense of release, rather than any active engagement in an exercise of wit or response to someone's joke. In her eyes, the laughter of Asian women functioned as a manifestation of their temporary escape from subservience—an antidote to what she conceived of as onerous "household duties" about to be imposed upon them once again, wrenching them away from "the fresh air," where she was sure they would rather have been. Their laughter was, in fact, a confirmation of their victimized status. And in "thinking about" these women's lives as burdened and burdensome, moreover, Townsend admitted that she was engaging in an act of imaginative projection, grounded in her own subjectivity: "I thought how difficult it must be to transplant yourself to a cold urban environment with a different set of rules and customs where the language is foreign . . . . I put myself in their place and knew that, were our positions to be reversed, I would go quietly mad" (Townsend, iii). The result of such projection was *The Great Celestial Cow,* a work in which Sita, the protagonist who had emigrated from a village in India to join her husband in Leicester, did indeed go insane at the climax—winding up imprisoned in a psychiatric hospital by her husband's family and committing suicide by leaping from a window.

Much of Townsend's play was comic in tone, finding humor in a woman's attempts to make herself understood in British culture, where her appearance, her manners, and her language all marked her as alien, and thus where she was perpetually misunderstood instead. Yet the only ending that Townsend could imagine for this comedy was a tragic one, with a heroine fated, so to speak, to go under. Destroyed by the strain of being subjected to merciless patriarchal authority within the Indian family and to racist xenophobia outside the home, Sita could do nothing but succumb to delusions and to suicidal impulses, in order to escape her plight.

Sue Townsend made clear through her Introduction to the play that she had retrospectively recast the spectacle she had witnessed of South Asian women laughing together. In order to serve as the starting-point for the work she wished to produce, it had to become a vision of figures who—as the poet Stevie Smith might have put it—were actually not waving, but drowning. Her own certainty that it would be impossible to maintain one's psychological integrity, as a South Asian dealing with life in Leicester, meant that these had to be women on the edge of breaking down, rather than finding a way to cope. Yet no attempt at empathy or desire to dramatize what would happen "were our positions to be reversed" seems ever to have led Townsend to consider the possibility of the opposite conclusion being true—that an Asian British woman of the 1980s might have been just as likely as Townsend herself to survive by laughing and by finding strength in fashioning alliances (particularly with her female peers), as well as in political activism. Indeed, the same snapshot-in-prose that Townsend had preserved of late-twentieth-century Asian life in England—a scene of women laughing openly in public, as a group—could have suggested an alternative and far more positive fate to a different viewer. This was not, after all, an image of a solitary figure going "quietly mad," but of women working together, staying noisily sane.

II

Against this background of heated disagreement, in which the subjectivity of Asian British women and thus their right to exercise and to interpret their own laughter was nearly as controversial a proposition—at least for some artists and audiences—as the subjectivity and laughter of the white, English New Woman had been one hundred years earlier, Suniti Namjoshi conceived her prose works of the 1980s. The title of the first volume to appear, *Feminist Fables,* was perhaps misleading. Its singling out of one genre may be responsible for the subsequent presumption, on the part of reviewers and journalists, that the literary fable must be, as Kausalya Santhanam has said, Namjoshi's "favourite form" (Santhanam, par. 12). Certainly, this 1981 volume contained many fables—reworkings, in some cases, of Western creations, such as those attributed to Aesops; in others, of tales from the *Panchatantra,* a collection of Sanskrit fables. But fables were just the beginning. In fact, Namjoshi ranged as widely in her appropriations and political refashionings of diverse literary predecessors as had Monique Wittig, in rewriting masculine literary history through the "feminaries" of her revolutionary *Les Guérillères* (1969), and as would Fay Weldon, in using William Blake's *The Marriage of Heaven and Hell,* G. B. Shaw's *Pygmalion,* Mary Shelley's *Frankenstein,* Milton's *Paradise Lost,* Hans Christian Andersen's "The Little Mermaid," and the Mills and Boon romance novels for her *The Life and Loves of a She-Devil* (1983).

Classical myths about the Greek gods; Viola and Olivia's relationship in Shakespeare's *Twelfth Night;* the stories of Sheherazade and of Haroun-al-Raschid from the *Arabian Nights;* the tales of transformation from Ovid's *Metamorphoses;* the legend of Guinevere from Malory's *Morte d'Arthur;* Chaucer's *The Wife of Bath's Tale* from *The Canterbury Tales;* the Creation narrative from the Old Testament; science-fiction adventure stories set on spaceships in far-off galaxies; Mother Goose nursery rhymes; the *Bhagavadgita*—these were just a few of the sources of material in *Feminist Fables.* To many of these, Namjoshi gave new twists that were not only political, but comic. Indeed, Namjoshi's short prose pieces made their arguments by generating laughter at the expense of the reader's assumptions about how the plots of these source narratives should proceed and at the cultural norms—whether racial, sexual, or class-based—that these texts formerly had been used to endorse. Her "fables" were polemical statements created through the medium of parody. This was parody as Linda Hutcheon has defined the term, embodying not "imitation" alone, but "repetition with critical distance, which marks difference rather than similarity" (Hutcheon, 6): an "integrated structural modeling process of revising, replaying, inverting, and 'trans-contextualizing' previous works of art" (Hutcheon, 11).

The particular works of art, in fact, to which Namjoshi turned quite often were not fables *per se,* but fairy tales from the Western tradition, especially those drawn from Charles Perrault's *Contes* and Hans Christian Andersen's *Fairy Tales.* In choosing to revise these fairy tales, she aligned herself with a mainstream feminist project that had been much in evidence since the early 1970s and the beginning of the Second Wave movement. Suniti Namjoshi's own efforts, therefore, joined hands with those of her white literary "sisters," such as Angela Carter and Joanna Russ, and with those of groups such as the Merseyside Fairy Story Collective, which contributed its 1972 rewriting of "Snow White" to Jack Zipes's influential collection, *Don't Bet on the Prince* (1987). In some ways, therefore, *Feminist Fables* laughed alongside and along with other feminist texts of the period and added its voice to communal political initiatives taking place through the medium of literature.

In a short prose piece such as "The Little Prince," for instance, Namjoshi showed herself at one with the general direction of feminist argument. Her variation on the conventional fairy tale about male accession to a throne and command over a kingdom emphasized, through ironic reversals, the lack of equality in opportunity still felt by those born female. Namjoshi's was a tale about an ironically-labelled "Wicked Stepmother," whose wickedness consisted of marrying a king and wanting their capable daughter, rather than his incompetent son by a previous union, to "reign alone" (Namjoshi, *Feminist Fables,* 15). In the course of the narrative, the young princess, who has been tutored in masculine pursuits, passes all the phallocentric tests for leadership ("hunting, drinking, tennis and mathematics, and a knowledge of the law," 15) to which the son cannot measure up. When the King reluctantly accedes, however, to his wife's request to give their daughter the governance of his realm, the public intervenes:

> Fortunately, the citizens had more sense. They all rose up as one man and yelled at the palace gates. "We will not be ruled by a woman." They hauled out the prince and set him on the throne. The wicked queen and her un-

> lucky daughter were exiled forever. And, thus, order was restored, and justice done. (15)

Namjoshi's comic touch asserted itself in this tale's narrative voice—a consistently ironic voice that underlined the stupidity and the offensiveness of misogyny by seeming to endorse its most appalling manifestations. Words such as "order" and "justice" became, in her hands, the punchlines of a cruel joke. It was a joke being played, however, not by the author on her characters, but by patriarchal institutions on the female audience beyond the text. Her story, therefore, invited readers to laugh along sympathetically with the point-of-view of Second Wave feminists, whose activism was grounded in premises such as the existence of systematic discrimination in the workplace, the presence of what later would be called a"glass ceiling" that effectively barred middle-class women's progress toward leadership, and the absence of a "level playing-field" for achievement.

But there was more to Suniti Namjoshi's choice of the fairy tale genre than a wish to contribute to the late-twentieth-century women's movement as it stood. Other concerns, too, including her allegiance to an earlier practitioner of it, drew her to this form. Namjoshi's approaches to rewriting the genre from a satirical angle, moreover, were different from those of her white literary contemporaries, as were her political goals. Although some of the *Feminist Fables* appeared to criticize the social order from a so-called "woman's" perspective, and thus to incorporate and leave undisturbed the notion that there was a body of experience shared by all women, others would turn their attention to the question of who was being shut out from current feminist definitions of "woman" and what their stories might look like. Namjoshi's narratives were not identical to those being produced by her peers; neither, in its emphasis upon difference rather than commonality, was her feminism the same as theirs.

We can begin to identify these differences between *Feminist Fables* and other works of the period by considering the utopian vision that informed the fairy tales published by many of Namjoshi's "sisters" in the women's movement. In his Introduction to *Don't Bet on the Prince,* which came after nearly two decades of such reworkings, Jack Zipes summed up the principles that had underpinned mainstream feminist revisions of the fairy tale:

> If we take the feminist tales for children and adults as a whole and generalise about their aesthetic and ideological features, we can see how closely

> they are related to feminist demands for gender rearrangement and equality in the family and at the work place. . . .
>
> The aesthetics of each individual tale depends on how each writer intends to explore the contradictions of gender antagonisms which are often linked to social problems. As we have seen, writers who address adults as primary audience tend to focus more on the conflicts between men and women and stress solidarity among women as the necessary first step to overcome the instrumental rationality of a male world. Ultimately, self-trust and trust of other women are the prerequisites for the creation of a new society. (Zipes, 32–3)

In other words, belief in the dream of universal sisterhood that still shaped much of the white women's movement of the 1970s and 1980s also underlay the literary manifestations of that movement. Feminist fairy tales, too, continued to "stress solidarity among women as the necessary first step," at the very moment when Black British women were asking, in the words of Hazel Carby, "[What] exactly do you mean when you say 'WE'??" (Carby, 52).

But Namjoshi's prose pieces continually exposed the fissures in that supposed solidarity. In her fairy tales, moreover, she used comedy of a painfully ironic and sometimes bitter sort to point out to her feminist readers when women themselves were responsible for these rifts, particularly through their own racism and homophobia. In doing so, she broke with some of her counterparts in the women's movement. As late as 1989, Paulina Palmer could still quote approvingly a statement from the British Women Against Violence Against Women group—better known by the initials "WAVAW"—that presented men as the antagonizing force between women and thus as the chief obstacle to female unity. According to WAVAW's formulation, the fashion industry, for instance—a male-dominated cultural institution—was responsible for turning women against one another:

> Under male supremacy women's status depends greatly on male approval. If we don't conform we pay heavy penalties . . . . Fashion divides us into angels, whores, dolly-birds, and hags. This is important in the maintenance of male power. It prevents us seeing each other as allies, but sets us up as enemies, always in competition. (Palmer, 33–4)

For Namjoshi, however, the question was not whether masculine interests had instigated hostility between and among women, but whether women themselves still embraced it and chose, moreover, to benefit from the existing divisions. Men might have given them the incentive to do so, but it was they who were climbing over the bodies of other women to advance within the already established hierarchy.

In her story "The Ugly One," Namjoshi preserved the structure of a fairy tale, beginning her narrative with the sentence, "Once upon a time there was an extraordinarily ugly creature," and ending it with a line labelled as the "Moral." What came between was a picture of the scapegoating of a figure whose "sex was indeterminate. . . . [though] after its death people generally agreed that it had once been a woman" (Namjoshi, *Feminist Fables,* 14). This figure "had tended to generate such extremes of disgust that, wholly without effort, she had, in the end, acquired a certain status," particularly as an object-lesson: "for people in general she became the Living Example of what they most genuinely did not want to become" (14). Throughout Namjoshi's story, the source of the supposed ugliness of this creature remained ambiguous, even as the narrative raised the possibility that it lay in her class status, for she was "poor" and, therefore, the "Spectre of Failure" for "hard-working men" (14). But the reference to her "indeterminate" gender, although she "had once been a woman" (as well as to her branding by "doctors and psychiatrists" as an "Unhealthy Aberration"), suggested an alternative construction of this hated figure—i. e., as lesbian. Such an allegorical reading cast in a different and disturbing light the reaction to her from "many little girls, and women also." For them, she had functioned as "Wholly Non-existent, except when they suffered from hideous nightmares" (14). They had turned her into a bogey, in order to assert their own normality.

Namjoshi, in other words, used her story "The Ugly One" to laugh both in sorrow and in anger at her heterosexist female contemporaries of the 1970s and 1980s for whom the lesbian was invisible and irrelevant, except as the image of what they most feared. If there was blame in this tale, it fell not only upon patriarchal institutions (such as Western medicine), but also upon individual heterosexual women, including those claiming a feminist identity. Such women were equally culpable for maintaining their own sense of cultural acceptability by designating others as fit only to be excluded and oppressed.

For Namjoshi, the comic fairy tale functioned less as an instrument for achieving "solidarity" and more as a medium for criticizing her audience and for addressing its misconduct with ironic laughter. Thus, her models for how to write in this genre were not necessarily drawn from her contemporaries' work. They appeared instead to have been taken from another, much earlier, source—often, from the late-Victorian fairy tales of Oscar Wilde, which had been published in volumes such as *The Happy Prince and Other Tales* (1888) and *A House of Pomegranates* (1891).

Why should Namjoshi have chosen to look back to Wilde? What could he mean to this woman from Bombay, born into a ruling-class family, who had held a post in the Indian Administrative Service, studied in the United States and Canada, become an academic with a teaching position in Toronto, spent a year in England, then later moved to Devon and settled there to live and write? Part of the explanation, perhaps, lay in the sympathy that Namjoshi felt with Oscar Wilde as a figure who had dealt earlier with both cultural and geographical displacement. An Irish gentleman who had dared to publish in England and to aim for precisely the success that had always been reserved for English-born gentleman, Wilde stood for the outsider who had stormed the gates, declared himself at home, and talked back both wittily and impudently to the insiders. For Namjoshi, who was publishing her works through feminist presses based in London and thus targeting British audiences, the confident and self-possessed voice with which Wilde spoke to English readers about themselves, especially in his satirical fairy tales, must have proved a useful guide.

But Wilde had a further and more deeply personal significance for her. In a brief autobiographical statement from 1989 for the *New Internationalist*, Namjoshi described the formative role that his history had played, during her adolescence in India, in her ability to name herself and her own desires:

> I was not aware of coming into contact with other homosexual people. But as a child I read a lot and was allowed to read whatever I liked. When I was about 13 or 14 years old I remember writing down on a piece of paper: "I think I am more likely to fall in love with a girl than with a boy. I think I like most of the women I know more than the men I know. Therefore I must be like Oscar Wilde". This was the only notion available to me at that time. (Namjoshi, "Writer," par. 2)

For someone growing up a culture that articulated no concept of lesbianism for her, the story of Oscar Wilde served as an anchor. Her knowledge of his sexuality gave her, at a crucial moment, both a way of constructing an identity for herself and of connecting such an identity with a life in the arts, particularly in literature.

Namjoshi's awareness, moreover, at that young age of Wilde's works and career suggests that what she probably had been reading were his fairy tales. Coming to his reworkings of the genre so early must have left a lasting impression, for the thematic links are obvious between a story such as "The Birthday of the Infanta" (published in *A House of Pomegranates*) and her own "The Ugly One," from *Feminist Fables*. Like Namjoshi's narrative, Wilde's had focused upon the unhappy, seemingly ineluctable fate of a "creature" both scorned and exploited for its "ugliness"—in this case, a young dwarf plucked from his rural home and delivered to the court of the Spanish Infanta—by those whose own sense of worth depends upon their power to define others as monstrous.

The inspiration that Wilde offered in terms of style, too, was especially pronounced in the deadpan comedy of his narrative voice, which ridiculed the values of his readers while seeming to echo them. In "The Devoted Friend" (from *The Happy Prince and Other Tales*) for instance, Wilde skewered his middle-class English audience's obsession with advancement in class status by showing a duck teaching her ducklings "how to stand on their heads in the water," as the prerequisite to entering "the best society" of water-fowl: "But the little ducks paid no attention to her. They were so young that they did not know what an advantage it is to be in society at all" (Wilde, 24). Surely Namjoshi had absorbed much from the irony of pronouncements such as these, which both turned back upon themselves and recoiled upon the reader, as she fashioned her own narrative commentary for *Feminist Fables* and resorted to similar mock endorsements of the very kinds of behavior she loathed.

But by the time of publishing *The Blue Donkey Fables* seven years later, in 1988, Suniti Namjoshi had largely moved away from the strategy of rewriting fairy tales in a Wildean mode, even as she had moved geographically closer to the audience that she wished to address. Having recently settled in England with her Australian-born partner, Gillian Hanscombe, Namjoshi evidently felt a new urgency to be direct and even confrontational with British readers, particularly over the issue of racism. Yet she maintained a comic framework, continuing to couch her narratives about human oppression in the medium of stories about talking animals. Such a framework could simultaneously deliver its punch and its punchline to the audience quite forcefully, but also allow a certain distance that would keep the message from offending.

Namjoshi was walking a narrow line. Like her "New Woman" predecessors one hundred years earlier, who could not afford to alienate completely the same male contemporaries whose ideology and behavior they wished to criticize, Namjoshi was castigating the very feminist colleagues with whom she would have to go on working. Her British publishers, in fact, were close allies of the women's movement, for the firms through which she issued her works in the 1980s—Sheba Feminist Publishers; the Women's Press; Jezebel Tapes and Books; Onlywomen Press, etc.—were founded and staffed by feminists. So, too, as an author who chose to publish through such presses, she could be sure that the majority of the customers buying her books were women who would have identified themselves as supporters of the movement. Comedy, therefore, offered the best vehicle to achieve the task before her. It contained the potential for bringing readers closer, allowing the writer to bind them intimately and amicably to the text and to earn their good will, while simultaneously exposing the oppressive behavior that she hoped to make them disavow. And indeed, Namjoshi proved more successful in shifting the paradigms of feminism through the laughter that she generated than the New Women had been in their attempts to reshape late-Victorian patriarchal institutions around them—a fact that may have owed something to the peculiarly favorable historical moment at which she was writing, as well as to the more receptive nature of the audience.

Certainly, by 1988, when Suniti Namjoshi issued *The Blue Donkey Fables,* white feminist readers were better prepared to laugh at and to renounce the old ideology of sisterhood than they might have been even a few years earlier. Not only had they witnessed that "universal" principle being challenged increasingly and by activist groups formed by British women of color, such as the Organization of Women of Asian and African Descent (or OWAAD), which had held national meetings annually in the early 1980s and had "set about the task of redefining. . . . [feminism] and claiming it for ourselves" (Bryan, Dadzie, and Scafe, 44); they had also seen it brought into question through their own observation of the larger British political scene. A woman now ran the nation, and she was no "sister."

If one of the standard propositions of post-suffrage feminist thought had always been that the election of women to public office would further the goal of equality, and that a female prime minister would necessarily champion women's rights, then the rise of Margaret Thatcher had laid waste to that assumption. With Thatcher's accession to power, the ideal of commonality and unity based on gender received its death-blow. She was, as Peter Clarke has written in *Hope and Glory: Britain, 1900–1990,* "often branded as a class warrior, for obvious reasons" (Clarke, 380); but in many respects, she was also a gender warrior, going into battle against the causes dear to the very women who had opened up equal access to the political sphere for her and for others. Looking back upon Thatcher's years in office from the vantage point of the late 1990s, Sheila Rowbotham would note somewhat acerbically that Thatcher "had little interest in women or in women's networks and was completely lacking in the ability to empathize imaginatively with women who neither resembled herself nor fitted her stereotypes" (Rowbotham, *A Century,* 480). But in 1988, while Thatcherism was still in full swing, Wendy Wasserstein, the American comic playwright, would put the matter less delicately: "I mean you just look at her and you want to put her panty hose on her head. I mean she's just, she's horrible" (Cohen, 267–8).

With Thatcher serving as an obvious reminder that not even white women were standing together in unity, Namjoshi was able to hit harder at her feminist readers for espousing a philosophy that was being discredited daily, knowing that they were ready for the blow. Namjoshi's emphasis upon the difference that race made began with the title of her 1988 volume, *The Blue Donkey Fables,* which brought color to the foreground. One of her sharpest satirical statements, however, on the topic of feminists, racism, white guilt, and attempts to co-opt Asian women as "sisters" for political purposes, while ignoring their own subjectivity, came in the short prose allegory called "The Sinner." In that narrative, the Blue Donkey, a professional writer "reciting some verse before an audience," is faced with the spectacle of "an ordinary grey donkey [who] marched up to her, fell at her feet and cried out in a loud voice, 'Sister, I have sinned! I seek absolution'" (Namjoshi, *Blue Donkey,* 36). Though the Blue Donkey, non-plussed at the rude disruption, objects "politely" that "'[There] must be some mistake. I am not your sister. Indeed, I don't think we've met . . . . You can't have sinned [against me],'" the grey donkey remains adamant. She insists that the "embarrassed" Blue Donkey must immediately demonstrate forgiveness of her, for "'I have been snotty and snobbish and often thought to myself that I despise blue donkeys and would never go near one or have one for a friend'" (36); but she now has decided that her past conduct was wrong and wants to be rewarded for her new magnanimity. The more that the Blue Donkey resists these self-serving demands for a public show of reconciliation, the more aggressive they grow: "'But you must listen. I've changed completely,' the grey donkey wailed. 'I believe in sisterhood. I'm going to be your friend.'" When it becomes clear to her that the Blue Donkey has no wish to be her "friend" on these terms, let alone her "sister," the grey donkey turns vicious: "'What? After everything I said? Who exactly do you think you are?'" (36). The narrative ends on a sourly comic note, with the Blue Donkey pushing her aside and suggesting that she go back to the other grey donkeys, to tell them "'that you excuse their greyness'" instead (36).

Namjoshi would press the same point home even harder in "Gracious Living," another of the political allegories from this volume of fables. This time, the protagonist of the tale would be not a Blue Donkey, but a "one-eyed monkey"—an animal, gendered as female, who quite literally wears her difference (including her difference from other monkeys) on her face. Namjoshi's monkey-figure, not a domestic creature herself, finds that she has been invited by the domesticated rabbits to visit their hutch in the farmyard. Even though "she didn't know the rabbits well," they have asked her to tea, an experience that turns out to be both awkward and frustrating for the monkey. Outside, hens circle the hutch, "clucking furiously" over their own exclusion from the "airy and comfortable" dwelling; "the one-eyed monkey said nothing, but she remembered that the ownership of the hutch had been controversial" (72). Inside, though greeted by all the rabbits with the words "'Welcome, Sister,'" the monkey, their token guest, is largely ignored by her hosts: "The rabbits talked among themselves, and every now and then—when it was possible—she put in a word" (72). They have asked her there, as it turns out, for a specific political reason:

> She turned to the rabbits. The eldest was addressing her. "We invited you to tea to ask you to join our organisation. All fellow creatures have certain problems in common."
>
> The one-eyed monkey didn't know what to say. She hated organisations; they involved meetings and committees and long discussions. "Ah, oh, well," she began, when one of the problems the rabbits had referred to manifested itself.
>
> "Quick! Run! Hide!" shrieked the rabbits . . .[and] before she knew it she had been bundled under a pile of leaves and four or five rabbits were sitting on her. (73)

The rabbits have hidden her out of fear that the farmer would see her there and punish them for associating with a member of a despised group. As an older rabbit explains after the danger has passed, "'If the humans had caught us consorting with monkeys . . . . They'd have thrown us out.'" "'And,'" as another one adds, "'the hens would have taken over'" (73). Thus the rabbits' behavior is circumscribed by the fear of losing their so-called privilege, which is nothing more than the privilege of living in a cage. One "intellectual" rabbit tells the monkey, "'You see, the really important thing is that the farmer musn't find out that we can unlock the hutch.'" The monkey responds disgustedly, "'The really important thing . . . is that you haven't found out what you can do once you have unlocked the hutch'" (73). As she leaves in anger, she sees the hens outside attempting to force their way into the door of the hutch—yet another group fighting not to be free, but to preserve its gilded cage of domestic oppression.

As an allegory of the then-current state of "sisterhood" in Britain, Namjoshi's narrative was unsparing. Its allegorical referents, moreover, operated on a number of levels, embracing not only conflicts in the women's movement of the 1980s that involved race and tokenism, but those generated by class difference, as well as by heterosexual feminists' "fear" of being seen "consorting" with lesbians and thus of losing the approval of men. That Namjoshi felt she could laugh her readers into seeking real liberation, rather than membership in groups conspiring to maintain their own oppression, said much about the trust that she placed not only in her feminist audience, but in comedy as a didactic method. Clearly, she believed that humor could, in some way, help to effect change.

And yet, like her counterparts among the "New Women" one hundred years earlier, she also knew better than to trust in the power of comic fiction alone. Laughter, however useful a strategy in some circumstances, was merely a beginning. Shortly after publishing *The Blue Donkey Fables,* she wrote in a brief journalistic piece in 1989 of the need that she had felt, over the course of a decade, for direct political action and, indeed, for organized movements within institutions:

> But I did not get into political activism—either feminism or gay liberation—until 1978 when I got to know an extremely intelligent and persuasive woman who used to wear Gay Liberation badges . . . . When I saw her getting abused and hurt for fighting my battle, so to speak, I felt ashamed of myself. I realized that politics was . . . really to do with personal ethics. After that I set up a Women's Studies programme at my college . . . . (Namjoshi, "Writer," par. 5)

III

"Is the interest in Indian writers in English a passing phase in England or have they established themselves not only among the intelligentsia but also among ordinary readers?" Suniti Namjoshi was asked by an interviewer for the newspaper *The Hindu* in 2000. Namjoshi's answer was non-committal, yet tinged with pessimism: "Ordinary people in England do not read, they watch TV . . . and those of us who like to read feel sad—but these changes are happening" (Santhanam, 3–4). A 1998 issue of the *Journal of Gender Studies*, published by the Hull Centre for Gender Studies, contained an article about South Asian women in East London that asserted confidently, "The present study demonstrates that there are significant changes taking place for South Asian women in contemporary British society" (Bhopal, 154). But the same issue also offered a more personal "Standpoint" piece by Sharmilla Beezmohum that spoke in less positive tones:

> Each time I stroll into a bookshop I am struck by the lack of good quality Black British writing . . . . I find myself searching in vain for any British Asian voices, particularly those of women. I begin to see this most invisible portion of the UK's ethnic minorities struggle to make themselves seen . . . young Asian women air their views on Asian discussion shows on the TV. Yet there is practically nothing in bookshops for me to read. It is a lonely and solitary existence—I so desperately want to read a . . . [text] written by someone who has had similar experiences to me, just for a change. (Beezmohum, 227)

The political comedy that Suniti Namjoshi published in the 1980s was not directed solely at white feminist audiences, nor did it serve merely to change the climate of the women's movement. It also spoke to and about South Asian women, especially those of the Indian diaspora, and provided them—whether they identified themselves as lesbian or as heterosexual—with a sense of encountering "similar experiences" to their own, "just for a change." It offered these Asian readers, too, at least a temporary sense of entering into a literary community—not the suspect "sisterhood" that the Second Wave women's movement had dangled before them, but something closer to what James F. English has described recently as part of post-structuralist feminism at the end of the twentieth century: A "*different* community, a community in and of difference, a community, as [Jean-Luc] Nancy expresses it, 'formed by an articulation of "particularities," and not founded in any autonomous essence that would subsist by itself and that would reabsorb or assume singular beings into itself'" (English, 23). If nothing else, it gave them the pleasure of a shared laugh.

But if British audiences in general may no longer be reading very much, Suniti Namjoshi herself may no longer be laughing as much either. In an extended memoir titled *Goja: An Autobiographical Myth* (2000), Namjoshi, who is now approaching the age of sixty, appears to have laid down what she had called, in a filmed interview for Pratibha Parmar's 1990 documentary,

Flesh and Paper, her earlier "weapons of wit . . . [and] sarcasm." Writing about the tragedies not only of her own life, including her childhood sexual abuse, but the tragedies of women such as Goja, the lower-caste servant who had looked after her in Bombay, Namjoshi seems to have turned away from the comic mode. Like Rebecca West before her, she has reached if not a disavowal of laughter, then at least an increased sense of its limitations and a reluctance to indulge in it without caution. What her latest text asks for and offers instead is a "blessing"—a blessing of "the world, and every living creature on it, every bird and beast there ever was"—but one that must inevitably be incomplete, so long as some lives are subject to poverty, oppression, and exploitation, and thus are unblessed (Namjoshi, *Goja,* 148).

Perhaps such a trajectory from the embrace of laughter to the rejection of it is inevitable. A comic perspective, it has been said, is particularly suited to the young, whose experiences with pain and loss are usually more limited. The history of women's comic fiction over the last one hundred years has displayed, again and again, a pattern of authors succumbing to growing doubts about the viability of the genre, especially as they move into the later stages of their careers and look backward. Laughter is the expression of those who are looking forward, regardless of chronological age.

What then can we say of the current state of British feminisms? Should the feminist movement today, made up of its many factions and constituencies, be called a thriving movement or a declining one? Is it just coming into its maturity, with all of its work before it, or is it now moribund? Where does it stand in its own life-cycle? Journalists and critics have searched everywhere for the signs that will tell them whether the forms of feminisms in evidence still represent a vital cause, pointed toward the future. The answer may lie not only in the obvious places—in the protests, the legislation, or the changes in consciousness that different varieties of feminism are inspiring—but in the sphere of creativity, whatever the medium. It may lie, in fact, in the comedies by women that feminist communities are still producing and still *hoping* to use to increase women's survival. If new generations of British women keep laughing together, and if laughter still rings through the movement, how can anyone believe that movement is drowning?

Works Cited

Ahmad, Rukhsana and Rahila Gupta, eds. *Flaming Spirit: Stories from the Asian Women Writers' Collective*. London: Virago, 1994.

Allen, Grant. *The Woman Who Did*. London: John Lane, 1895.

Aptheker, Bettina. *Tapestries of Life: Women's Work, Women's Consciousness, and the Meaning of Daily Experience*. Amherst: U of Massachusetts P, 1989.

Ardis, Ann L. *New Women, New Novels: Feminism and Early Modernism*. New Brunswick, NJ: Rutgers U P, 1990.

Baker, Niamh. *Happily Ever After? Women's Fiction in Postwar Britain, 1945–1960*. London: Macmillan, 1989.

Barreca, Regina, ed. *Last Laughs: Perspectives on Women and Comedy*. New York: Gordon and Breach, 1988.

———, ed. *New Perspectives on Women and Comedy*. Philadelphia: Gordon and Breach, 1992.

———, ed. *The Penguin Book of Women's Humor*. New York: Penguin, 1996.

———. *They Used to Call Me Snow White . . . But I Drifted*. New York: Viking, 1991.

Baumgardner, Jennifer and Amy Richards. *Manifesta: Young Women, Feminism, and the Future*. New York: Farrar, Straus and Giroux, 2000.

Bayley, John. "Where, Exactly, Is the Pym World?" *The Life and Work of Barbara Pym*. Ed. Dale Salwak. Iowa City: U of Iowa P, 1987. 50–57.

Beezmohum, Sharmilla. "Where Are All the British Asian Writers." *Journal of Gender Studies* 7. 2 (1998): 227.

Berger, Joseph. "The 'Second Generation' Reflects on the Holocaust." *New York Times*. 17 January 2000, Washington final ed.: A11+.

Bhaji on the Beach. Screenplay by Meera Syal. Dir. Gurinder Chadha. Film Four International, UMBI Films Production, 1993.

Bhopal, Kalwant. "South Asian Women in East London: Religious Experience and Diversity." *Journal of Gender Studies* 7. 2 (1998): 143–56.

"Bibliography." *Rebecca West: A Celebration. With a Critical Introduction by Samuels Hynes*. New York: Viking, 1977. 761–6.

Bjørhovde, Gerd. *Rebellious Structures: Women Writers and the Crisis of the Novel, 1880–1900.* Oslo: Norwegian U P, 1987.

Blythe, Ronald. Introduction. *Emma.* By Jane Austen. New York: Penguin, 1966.

Brantly, Susan. *The Life and Writings of Laura Marholm.* Beiträge zur nordischen Philologie, Bd. 21. Basel and Frankfurt am Main: Helbing & Lichtenhahn Verlag AG, 1991.

Brief Encounter. Screenplay by Anthony Havelock-Allan, David Lean, and Ronald Neame. Dir. David Lean. Cineguild. 1945.

Briggs, Julia. *A Woman of Passion: The Life of E. Nesbit, 1858–1924.* London: Hutchinson, 1987.

Brittain, Vera. *Testament of Youth.* 1933. N. p.: Wideview, 1980.

Brookner, Anita. "The Bitter Fruits of Rejection." *The Spectator.* 19 July 1986. 30–31.

———. *Family and Friends.* New York: Pantheon, 1985.

———. *Fraud.* London: Jonathan Cape, 1992.

———. *Hotel du Lac.* London: Jonathan Cape, 1984.

———. *Latecomers.* London: Jonathan Cape, 1988.

———. *Look at Me.* New York: Pantheon, 1983.

Bryan, Beverley, Stella Dadzie, and Suzanne Scafe. "The Heart of the Race: Black Women's Lives in Britain." 1985. *Black British Feminism: A Reader.* Ed. Heidi Safia Mirza. London: Routledge, 1997. 42–4.

Burney, Fanny. *Evelina, or the History of a Young Lady's Entrance into the World.* 1778. Ed. Edward A. Bloom. Oxford: Oxford U P, 1982.

Carby, Hazel. "White Woman Listen! Black Feminism and the Boundaries of Sisterhood." 1982. *Black British Feminism: A Reader.* Ed. Heidi Safia Mirza. London: Routledge, 1997. 45–53.

Carlson, Susan. *Women and Comedy: Rewriting the British Theatrical Tradition.* Ann Arbor: U of Michigan P, 1991.

Cheyette, Bryan. Introduction. *Contemporary Jewish Writing in Britain and Ireland: An Anthology.* London: Peter Halban, 1998. xiii–lxxi.

Churchill, Winston S. "Earl Haig." *The Legion Book.* Ed. Captain H. Cotton Minchin. London: Cassell and Co., 1929. 21–2.

Cixous, Hélène. "The Laugh of the Medusa." Trans. Keith Cohen and Paula Cohen. *The Signs Reader: Women, Gender, and Scholarship.* Eds. Elizabeth Abel and Emily K. Abel. Chicago: U of Chicago P, 1983. 279–97.

Clarke, Peter. *Hope and Glory: Britain 1900–1990.* The Penguin History of Britain IX. London: Penguin, 1996.

Cohen, Esther. "Uncommon Woman: An Interview with Wendy Wasserstein." *Last Laughs: Perspectives on Women and Comedy.* Ed. Regina Barreca. New York: Gordon and Breach, 1988. 257–70.

Coward, Noel. *Blithe Spirit. Three Plays.* New York: Grove Press, 1965. 7–109.

———. *Private Lives. Three Plays.* New York: Grove Press, 1965. 181–254.

Crawford, Mary. "Just Kidding: Gender and Conversational Humor." *New Perspectives on Women and Comedy.* Ed. Regina Barreca. Philadelphia: Gordon and Breach, 1992. 23–37.

D'Arcy, Ella. "The Pleasure-Pilgrim." Monochromes. London: John Lane, Vigo St[.], 1895. 129–75.

Deakin, Motley F. *Rebecca West.* Twayne's English Authors Series, 296. Boston: G. K. Hall, 1980.

Debelius, Margaret. "Countering a Counterpoetics: Ada Leverson and Oscar Wilde." *Women and British Aestheticism.* Eds. Talia Schaffer and Kathy Alexis Psomiades. Charlottesville: U Press of Virginia, 1999. 192–210.

DeKoven, Marianne. *Rich and Strange: Gender, History, and Modernism.* Princeton: Princeton U P, 1991.

Delaney, Shelagh. *A Taste of Honey: A Play.* New York: Grove Weidenfeld, 1959.

Dixon, Ella Hepworth. *As I Knew Them: Sketches of People I Have Met on the Way.* London: Hutchinson & Co, 1930.

———. "A Literary Lover." *The Woman's World.* 3. London: Cassell & Co., 1890: 638–41.

———. *My Flirtations.* By Margaret Wynman. London: Chatto & Windus, 1892.

———. *The Story of a Modern Woman.* New York: Cassell, 1894.

Edson, Evelyn. "This Time, It's Funny: Feminism and Humor." *Iris: A Journal About Women* 20 (Fall/Winter 1988): 31–3.

Egerton, George [Mary Chavelita Dunne Bright]. *The Backsliders.* 1911. TS. 948711. Theatre Collection, New York Public Library, New York, N. Y.

———. *Keynotes.* London: Elkin Mathews and John Lane, 1893.

———. "Virgin Soil." *Discords.* London: John Lane, 1894. 145–62.

———. *The Wheel of God.* London: Grant Richards, 1899.

Ellmann, Richard. *Oscar Wilde.* London: Hamish Hamilton, 1987.

English, James F. *Comic Transactions: Literature, Humor, and the Politics of Community in Twentieth-Century Britain.* Ithaca and London: Cornell U P, 1994.

Epstein, Helen. *Children of the Holocaust: Conversations with Sons and Daughters of Survivors.* New York: G. P. Putnam's Sons, 1979.

Fisher-Wirth, Ann. "Hunger Art: The Novels of Anita Brookner." *Twentieth Century Literature* 41.1 (1995): 1–15.

Fleming, George [Julia Constance Fletcher]. "For Better, For Worse." *Little Stories About Women.* London: Grant Richards, 1897. 193–206.

Flesh and Paper: A Film by Pratibha Parmar. Dir. Pratibha Parmar. Hyphen Films for Channel Four Television, U. K. 1990.

Forster, E. M. *Howards End.* 1910. Vintage Books, V-7. New York: Random House, n.d.

———. *A Passage to India.* 1924. San Diego and New York: Harcourt Brace Jovanovich, n. d.

———. *A Room with a View.* 1908. New York: Vintage, n. d.

Frye, Northrop. *Anatomy of Criticism: Four Essays.* Princeton: Princeton U P, 1957.

Gaskell, Elizabeth. *Cranford.* 1853. Ed. Elizabeth Porges Watson. Oxford: Oxford U P, 1980.

The Ghost and Mrs. Muir. Screenplay by Philip Dunne. Dir. Joseph L. Mankiewicz. Twentieth Century Fox, 1947.

Gilbert, Sandra M. and Susan Gubar. *The War of the Words.* Vol. I of *No Man's Land: The Place of the Woman Writer in the Twentieth Century.* 3 vols. New Haven: Yale U P, 1987.

Gissing, George. *Charles Dickens: A Critical Study.* London: Blackie & Son, 1898.

Glendinning, Victoria. *Rebecca West: A Life.* London: Weidenfeld and Nicolson, 1987.

Goodman, Lizbeth. "Gender and Humour." *Imagining Women: Cultural Representations and Gender.* Eds. Frances Bonner, Lizbeth Goodman, Richard Allen, Linda Janes, and Catherine King. Cambridge: Polity, 1992. 286–300.

Grafe, Frieda. *The Ghost and Mrs. Muir.* BFI Film Classics. London: British Film Institute, 1995.

Gray, Frances. *Women and Laughter.* Charlottesville: U P of Virginia, 1994.

Guppy, Shusha. "The Art of Fiction XCVIII: Anita Brookner." *Paris Review* 29 (1987): 147–69.

Haffenden, John. "Anita Brookner." *Novelists in Interview.* London: Methuen, 1985. 57–75.

Hamilton, Cicely and "Christopher St[.] John" (Christabel Marshall). *How the Vote Was Won. How the Vote Was Won, and Other Suffragette Plays.* Researched by Candida Lacey. Introduced by Dale Spender. With Notes for Performance by Carole Hayman. New York and London: Methuen, 1985. 22–33.

Hardy, Thomas. *Jude the Obscure.* 1896. New York: Penguin, 1978.

Heilmann, Ann. *New Woman Fiction: Women Writing First-Wave Feminism.* London: Macmillan, 2000.

Hutcheon, Linda. *Theory of Parody: The Teachings of Twentieth-Century Art Forms.* New York and London: Methuen, 1985.

Hutchinson, G. Evelyn. *A Preliminary List of the the Writings of Rebecca West: 1912–1951.* New Haven: Yale U P, 1957.

Inness, Sherrie A. "Introduction: Girl Problems." *Running for Their Lives: Girls, Cultural Identity, and Stories of Survival.* Lanham, MD and Oxford: Rowman and Littlefield, 2000.

Isaak, Jo Anna. *Feminism and Contemporary Art: The Revolutionary Power of Women's Laughter.* London: Routledge, 1996.

Kaplan, Deborah. *Jane Austen Among Women.* Baltimore and London: The Johns Hopkins U P, 1992.

Kaufman, Gloria. Introduction. *Pulling Our Own Strings: Feminist Humor and Satire.* Eds. Gloria Kaufman and Mary Kay Blakely. Bloomington: Indiana U P, 1980. 13–16.

———. "Introduction: Humor and Power." *In Stitches: A Patchwork of Feminist Humor and Satire.* Ed. Gloria Kaufman. Bloomington and Indianapolis: Indiana U P, 1991. vii–xii.

Kazi, Najma. "Conflict." *Sojourn.* Ed. Zhana. London: Methuen, 1988.

Keane, Molly. *Devoted Ladies.* By M. J. Farrell. 1934. London: Virago, 1984.

Kemp, Sandra and Judith Squires. "Epistemologies: Introduction." *Feminisms.* Oxford: Oxford U P, 1997. 142–5.

Kenyon, Olga. "Anita Brookner." *Women Writers Talk: Interviews with 10 Women Writers.* New York: Carroll & Graf, 1990. 8–24.

Koonz, Claudia. "Consequences: Women, Nazis, and Moral Choice." *Different Voices: Women and the Holocaust.* Eds. Carol Rittner and John Roth. New York: Paragon House, 1993. 288–308.

Kranidis, Rita S. *Subversive Discourse: The Cultural Production of Late Victorian Feminist Novels.* New York: St. Martin's, 1995.

Kremer, S. Lillian. *Women's Holocaust Writing: Memory and Imagination.* Lincoln: U of Nebraska P, 1999.

Kureishi, Yasmin. "Reworking Myths: Sutapa Biswas." *Visibly Female. Feminism and Art: An Anthology.* Ed. Hilary Robinson. London: Camden, 1987.

Kushner, Tony. *The Holocaust and the Liberal Imagination: A Social and Cultural History.* Oxford: Blackwell, 1994.

Lawrence, C. E. "Wanted—Humourists." *The Book Monthly.* (London) May 1906: 549–52.

Ledger, Sally. "The New Woman and the Crisis of Victorianism." *Cultural Politics at the Fin de Siècle.* Eds. Sally Ledger and Scott McCracken. Cambridge: Cambridge U P, 1995. 22–44.

———. *The New Woman: Fiction and Feminism at the Fin de Siècle.* Manchester, UK: Manchester U P, 1997.

Leslie, Josephine Campbell. *The Ghost and Mrs. Muir.* By R. A. Dick. New York: Ziff-Davis, 1945.

———. *Unpainted Portrait.* By R. A. Dick. London: Hodder and Stoughton, 1954.

Lewis, Jane. "Myrdal, Klein, *Women's Two Roles* and Postwar Feminism 1945–1960." *British Feminism in the Twentieth Century.* Ed. Harold L. Smith. Amherst, MA: U of Massachusetts P, 1990. 167–88.

Lewis, Paul. *Comic Effects: Interdisciplinary Approaches to Humor in Literature.* Albany, NY: State U of New York P, 1989.

Lorde, Audre. "The Master's Tools Will Never Dismantle the Master's House." *This Bridge Called My Back: Writings of Radical Women of Color.* Eds. Cherrie Moraga and Gloria Anzaldua. New York: Kitchen Table, 1983. 98–101.

Marholm Hansson, Laura. *Modern Women: An English Rendering of Laura Marholm Hansson's 'Das Buch der Frauen' by Hermione Ramsden.* London: John Lane, The Bodley Head, 1896.

———. *We Women and Our Authors.* Trans. Hermione Ramsden. London: John Lane, The Bodley Head, 1899.

Marks, Patricia. *Bicycles, Bangs, and Bloomers: The New Woman in the Popular Press.* Lexington, KY: U P of Kentucky, 1990.

McGifford, Diane. "Suniti Namjoshi (1941–)." *Writers of the Indian Diaspora: A Bio-Bibliographical Critical Sourcebook.* Ed. Emmanuel S. Nelson. Westport, CT: Greenwood, 1993. 291–7.

Meredith, George. "The Case of General Ople and Lady Camper." *Loves and Deaths: Novelists' Tales of the Nineteenth-Century: from Scott to Hardy.* Ed. Peter Bayley. Oxford: Oxford U P, 1972. 213–65.

———. "An Essay on Comedy." 1877. *Comedy: "An Essay on Comedy" by George Meredith and "Laughter" by Henri Bergson.* Ed. Wylie Sypher. Baltimore: The Johns Hopkins U P, 1980. 3–57.

Meynell, Alice. *Ceres' Runaway and Other Essays.* London: Constable, 1909.

———. *The Colour of Life and Other Essays on Things Seen and Heard.* London: John Lane, 1896.

———. "Dickens." *Alice Meynell, Prose and Poetry: Centenary Volume.* Eds. F. P. [Frederick Page], V. M. [Viola Meynell], O. S. [Olivia Meynell] & F. M. [Francis Meynell]. London: Jonathan Cape, 1947, 108–22.

———. *The Rhythm of Life and Other Essays.* London: Elkin Mathews and John Lane, 1893.

Mirza, Heidi Safia. "Introduction: Mapping a Genealogy of Black British Feminism." *Black British Feminism: A Reader.* Ed. Heidi Safia Mirza. Routledge: London, 1997. 1–28.

Namjoshi, Suniti. *The Blue Donkey Fables.* London: The Women's Press, 1988.

———. *The Conversations of Cow.* London: The Women's Press, 1985.

———. *Feminist Fables.* 1981. London: Sheba Feminist Publishers, 1990.

———. *Goja: An Autobiographical Myth.* North Melbourne, Australia: Spinifex, 2000.

———. "Writer—Suniti Namjoshi." "Pride and Prejudice: Homosexuality." *New Internationalist* 201 (November 1989). 14 July 2000. <http: // www.oneworld.org/ni/issue 201/terrace.htm>.

Natarajan, Nalini, "Introduction: Reading Diaspora." *Writers of the Indian Diaspora: A Bio-Bibliographical Critical Sourcebook.* Ed. Emmanuel S. Nelson. Westport, CT: Greenwood, 1993. xiii–xix.

Nesbit, E. [Edith]. "Acting for the Best." *In Homespun.* London: John Lane, Vigo St[.], 1896. 104–24.

———. *A Pomander of Verse.* London: John Lane at The Bodley Head, 1895.

Orel, Harold. *The Literary Achievement of Rebecca West.* New York: St. Martin's, 1986.

Palmer, Paulina. *Contemporary Women's Fiction: Narrative Practice and Feminist Theory.* Hemel Hempstead: Harvester Wheatsheaf, 1989.

Parmar, Pratibha. "That Moment of Emergence." *Feminism and Film.* Ed. E. Ann Kaplan. Oxford Readings in Feminism. Oxford: Oxford U P, 2000. 375–83.

Paston, George [Emily Morse Symonds]. *A Writer of Books.* 1898. Chicago: Academy Chicago, 1999.

Pugh, Martin. "Domesticity and the Decline of Feminism, 1930–1950." *British Feminism in the Twentieth Century.* Ed. Harold L. Smith. Amherst, MA: U of Massachusetts P, 1990. 144–64.

Pykett, Lynn. *The "Improper" Feminine: The Women's Sensation Novel and the New Woman Writing*. London and New York: Routledge, 1992.

———. "Portraits of the Artists as a Young Woman: Representations of the Female Artist in the New Woman Fiction of the 1890s." *Victorian Women Writers and the Woman Question.* Ed. Nicola Diane Thompson. Cambridge: Cambridge U P, 1999. 135–50.

Pym, Barbara. *Excellent Women.* 1952. New York: Harper and Row, 1980.

———. *An Unsuitable Attachment*. New York: E. P. Dutton, 1982.

Rich, Adrienne. "Disloyal to Civilization: Feminism, Racism and Gynephobia." *On Lies, Secrets and Silence: Selected Essays, 1966–1978.* New York: W. W. Norton & Co., 1979. 275–310.

Richardson, Angelique and Chris Willis, eds. *The New Woman in Fiction and in Fact: Fin-de-Siècle Feminisms*. Houndmills, Basingstoke: Palgrave, 2001.

Rickett, Arthur. *Lost Chords.* London: A. D. Innes, 1895.

Rollyson, Carl. *The Literary Legacy of Rebecca West.* Bethesda, MD: International Scholars Publications, 1998.

———. *Rebecca West: A Saga of the Century.* London: Hodder and Stoughton, 1995.

Rowbotham, Sheila. *A Century of Women: The History of Women in Britain and the United States.* New York: Viking, 1997.

———.*Woman's Consciousness, Man's World.* Harmondsworth: Penguin, 1973.

Rutledge, Amelia A. "E. Nesbit and the Woman Question." *Victorian Woman Writers and the Woman Question.* Ed. Nicola Diane Thompson. Cambridge: Cambridge UP, 1999. 223–40.

[Santhanam, Kausalya]. "Feminism, One of Her Voices." *The Hindu on Indiaserver.* 20 February 2000. 14 July 2000. <http://www.the-hindu.com/2000/02/20/stories/1320129u.htm>.

Sackville-West, Vita. Introduction. *Alice Meynell, Prose and Poetry: Centenary Volume.* Eds. F.P. [Frederick Page], V. M. [Viola Meynell], O. S. [Olivia Meynell] & F. M. [Francis Meynell]. London: Jonathan Cape, 1947. 7–26.

Sadler, Lynn Veach. *Anita Brookner.* Twayne's English Authors Series. Boston: G. K. Hall, 1990.

Schaffer, Talia. *Forgotten Female Aesthetes: Literary Culture in Late-Victorian England.* Charlottesville: U of Virginia P, 2000.

Scott, Bonnie Kime. *Refiguring Modernism: Postmodern Feminist Readings of Woolf, West, and Barnes.* Vol. II. Bloomington: Indiana U P, 1995.

———. Introduction. *Selected Letters of Rebecca West.* New Haven: Yale U P, 2000. xv–xxiv.

Severin, Laura. *Stevie Smith's Resistant Antics.* Madison: U of Wisconsin P, 1997.

Shaw, [George] Bernard. *Heartbreak House: A Fantasia in the Russian Manner on English Themes. Selected Plays.* 1917. Vol. I. New York: Dodd, Mead and Co., n. d. 447–598.

Showalter, Elaine. *Sexual Anarchy: Gender and Culture at the Fin de Siècle.* New York: Viking Press, 1990.

Skinner, John. *The Fictions of Anita Brookner: Illusions of Romance.* New York: St. Martin's, 1992.

Staves, Susan. "*Evelina*; or, Female Difficulties." *Fanny Burney's Evelina.* Ed. Harold Bloom. Modern Critical Interpretations. New York: Chelsea House, 1988. 13–30.

Stetz, Margaret [Diane]. "Anita Brookner: Woman Writer as Reluctant Feminist." *Writing the Woman Artist: Essays on Poetics, Politics, and Portraiture.* Ed. Suzanne W. Jones. Philadelphia: U of Pennsylvania P, 1991. 96–112.

———. "Drinking 'The Wine of Truth' Philosophical Change in West's *Return of the Soldier.*" *Arizona Quarterly* 43. 1 (1987): 63–78.

———. "Ella Hepworth Dixon." *Late-Victorian and Edwardian British Novelists, Second Series.* Ed. George M. Johnson. *Dictionary of Literary Biography.* Vol. 197. Detroit: Gale Research, 1999. 99–109.

———. "Life's 'Half-Profits': Writers and Their Readers in Fiction of the 1890s." *Nineteenth-Century Lives: Essays Presented to Jerome Hamilton Buckley.* Eds. Laurence S. Lockridge, John Maynard, and Donald D. Stone. Cambridge: Cambridge U P, 1989. 169–87.

Stevenson, John. *British Society, 1914–45.* The Pelican Social History of Britain. Harmondsworth: Penguin, 1984.

Stewart, James McG. *Rudyard Kipling: A Bibliographical Catalogue.* Ed. A. W. Yeats. Toronto: Dalhousie U P and U of Toronto P, 1959.

Syrett, Netta. *Nobody's Fault.* London: John Lane, 1896.

Townsend, Sue. *The Great Celestial Cow.* London: Methuen, 1990.

Vincent, Sybil Korff. "The Mirror and the Cameo: Margaret Atwood's Comic/Gothic Novel." *The Female Gothic.* Ed. Juliann E. Fleenor. Montreal: Eden Press, 1983. 153–63.

Walker, Nancy. *A Very Serious Thing: Women's Humor and American Culture.* Minneapolis: U of Minnesota P, 1988.

Weldon, Fay. *The Life and Loves of a She-Devil.* New York: Ballantine, 1983.

Wells, H. G. *The War of the Worlds.* 1898. Afterwd. Isaac Asimov. New York: New American Library, 1986.

West, Rebecca. *Black Lamb and Grey Falcon.* Vol. I. London: Macmillan, 1942.

———. *The Court and the Castle: A Study of the Interactions of Political and Religious Ideas in Imaginative Literature.* London: Macmillan, 1958.

———. *Cousin Rosamund.* London: Macmillan, 1985.

———. "Elegy." *The Legion Book.* Ed. Captain H. Cotton Minchin. London: Cassell and Co, 1929. 183–91.

———. *Ending in Earnest: A Literary Log.* Garden City, NY: Doubleday, Doran & Co, 1931.

———. *Family Memories.* London: Virago, 1987.

———. *The Fountain Overflows.* 1956. New York: Penguin, 1985.

———. *Harriet Hume: A London Fantasy.* London: Hutchinson & Co., 1929.

———. *The Return of the Soldier.* 1918. New York: Penguin, 1998.

———. *This Real Night.* London: Macmillan, 1984.

Wilde, Oscar. *Complete Short Fiction.* Ed. Ian Small. London: Penguin, 1994.

Wittig, Monique. *Les Guérillères.* Trans. David LeVay. New York: Viking, 1969.

Wolfe, Peter. *Rebecca West: Artist and Thinker.* Carbondale, IL: Southern Illinois U P, 1971.

Woolf, Virginia. *Between the Acts.* London: The Hogarth Press, 1941.

———. *Orlando: A Biography.* 1928. San Diego and New York: Harcourt Brace Jovanovich, n. d.

———. "Professions for Women." *The Death of the Moth and Other Essays.* New York: Harcourt Brace Jovanovich, 1974. 235–42.

Zhana, ed. *Sojourn.* London: Methuen, 1988.

Zipes, Jack. Introduction. *Don't Bet on the Prince: Contemporary Feminist Fairy Tales in North America and England.* 1987. rpt. New York: Routledge, 1989. 1–36.

Index